Jesus, Me, & Afternoon Tea

A Devotional and 'Afternoon Tea'
Cookbook and Fun Facts
About Your Favorite Teas

DEANNA L STALNAKER

KARDEE'S ANGEL PUBLISHING

ISBN: 0989426769
ISBN 13: 9780989426763
Library of Congress Control Number: 2014909248
LCCN Imprint Name: KarDee's Angel Publishing, Tobaccoville, NC

*Dedicated to all my friends
and family who love Jesus, tea and food! God bless you all
and I pray that you will always
find a quiet place of peace and rest
while you enjoy reading and meditating on the love of God
and drinking a warm and comforting
cup of tea.*

Table of Contents

Introduction

*And God said, 'Let the earth bring forth grass, the herb
yielding seed, and the fruit tree yielding fruit after his kind,
whose seed is in itself, upon the earth': and it was so.*
GENESIS 1:11

...And God saw that it was good.
GENESIS 1:12B

THE WORLD IS A BEAUTIFUL PLACE AND GOD gives us all things to enjoy.
He knew when he created the world that we would have times when
we needed to get alone by ourselves in quiet contemplation, gather with
our friends in celebration, or just enjoy a time of special fellowship with
one another.... so he created tea.

The purpose of this book is to share verses, short anecdotes or devotions,
recipes for various types of teas and other delicious goodies to go with your
afternoon teas, whether you are spending a time of quiet and solitude with
just your own thoughts or having an elaborate get-together with your friends.
In this book you will also take a short trip through history from the discovery
of tea through today when tea is rapidly becoming the number one drink of
people everywhere. You will also learn about the calming and medicinal benefits of your favorite drink as you explore the various types of teas and herbs.

So indulge yourself. Get out your best china, pour the tea, gather
the snacks, get your Bible or devotional book, and take them all to your
favorite comfortable chair or gather your friends together and enjoy the
fellowship of Jesus, Me, and Afternoon Tea.

The History of Tea

LEGEND HAS IT THAT TEA TRADITIONALLY HAD ITS beginnings in China in 2737 BC. Emperor Sh'eng Nung, an herbalist and scholar, was resting from his journey he was taking to the distant part of his realm with his servants. He was sitting under a tree, drinking a cup of hot water (for hygienic purposes he boiled his water before he drank it). While he was resting there, a few of the dried leaves from the tree above him fell into the water. The boiling water turned a light golden brown and smelled invigorating and tasted refreshing. He found that after he drank it, he was energized and was able to continue his journey. Whether this was legend or the truth, tea was known to exist and to be drunk this early in history in China and became a popular drink there around that time.

The first written history of tea occurred in the third century BC when a Chinese doctor recommended it for increasing alertness, stamina, and concentration. The first term used as a name for this drink was the Chinese character 'tu'. Sometime later between 206 BC and 220 AD they started using the pronunciation 'cha' to refer to tea. During this time in Chinese culture, cha was the favorite drink across all levels of society. In 800 AD Lu Yu wrote the first book about tea called 'Cha Ching'.

With the increasing popularity of tea as both a drink and a medicinal tonic, farmers in Southeast Asia began to cultivate the trees on their land. They explored special drying techniques and learned to compress the tealeaves into cakes. These cakes made it an easy way to be stored and bartered with other countries. They were given as gifts to their leaders or emperors and later, as the supply of tea grew and the drink became even more popular, it started to show up in taverns, markets, and noodle houses, making it readily accessible to everyone.

Tea merchants became rich and potters and goldsmiths began making beautiful vessels in which to serve the tea.

Around 500 AD, Prince Siddhartha, the Indian prince who would become the Buddha, traveled to the Far East in search of enlightenment. He pledged to stay awake for nine years to meditate and learn, but after five years he became very sleepy. He happened upon a bush and started chewing a few of its leaves. He found that after chewing on them he became more alert and energetic. Later he learned that the leaves were from a tea plant. When he returned to India, he brought with him some seeds of this amazing plant so that the farmers could cultivate it in his country. Later on, in the mid 1800's, India would become the largest tea-growing country in the world.

About 300 years later a Buddhist monk from Japan, Dengyo Daishi, happened to be studying in China. While he was in China, he noticed that the monks who had drunk the tea were more alert and were able to stay awake longer during their prayers and meditation. He wanted to bring the tea back to Japan. In 1211, another Buddhist monk, whose name was Eisai, wrote a book called 'Maintaining Health by Drinking Tea'. In the book he describes the benefits of drinking tea. The monks began using tea in their spiritual ceremonies. The following is the 'Five Theories of the Japanese Tea Ceremony (Chanoyu)':

- *Wa: stands for harmony. There is harmony in nature.*
- *Kei: stands for respect. Guests must respect all things.*
- *Sei: stands for purity. Upon entering the tearoom, one is to leave behind their worries of daily life.*
- *Jaku: stands for tranquility. This is only achieved after the first three steps are achieved.*
- *Wabi: appreciating the beauty of things that are simple and natural.*

By the end of the sixth century, tea was widely introduced to the rest of Asia by the traveling Zen Buddhist monks.

Tea was primarily an Asian brew until late in the 1500 and 1600's. The first mention of tea in Europe was in 1559 in a book called 'Voyages and Travels' by a Venetian sailor and writer. In it are the words 'chai catai' which means 'tea of China'. In 1615, R.L. Wickham of the English East India Company was the first to mention tea in England's literature.

It's unclear whether it was the Dutch or Portuguese who first introduced tea to Europe. They were both trading in Southeast Asia at the time. Among their imports were included some of the teas they found in the markets during their travels. By the mid 1600's, they were bringing Chinese and Japanese teas in their cargoes. From the first introduction of tea in Europe, it became very popular among all the classes, especially in Holland. Its popularity grew less in Germany and France, with the exception of some of their regions. The Dutch provided the first restaurant service with tea.

Tea reached the nobility in Russia in 1618 when the Chinese gave a gift of tea to Tsar Alexis. Later a trade agreement was made in 1689. It took many months for them to transport the tea over land by caravan. It was very expensive and so only the aristocrats could afford it. Later when the supplies became more plentiful, the price went down and it became a popular drink there with all the people.

The first recorded date of tea being in England was 1658. Thomas Garraway, a local merchant in London, advertised the Chinese drink in the weekly London newspaper. A couple of years later he advertised the drink as something that would cure almost any known ailment. Later in 1662, King Charles II, married a Portuguese princess, Catharine of Braganza. She was an avid tea drinker and brought a large supply with her as part of her dowry. She often served it to her friends and later on, word had gotten around about how good it was and others wanted to try it for themselves. At this time, tea continued to be expensive and it was mainly a drink for the aristocracy and wealthy businessmen and politicians. When all classes of people started to drink it and demands for the drink had started going up, a smuggling and black market business from Holland developed. Politicians and priests were among those who were involved in the illicit trade. To make more profit, they increased the yield of tea by adding other leaves to it (licorice and sloe). Used leaves were reprocessed with molasses or clay and other questionable staining techniques.

During the eighteen century tea became the most popular drink in England. It was drunk at all times of the day. Tea gardens had started to spring up throughout Great Britain. These were beautiful gardens where people could enjoy drinking their tea outdoors. People from all walks of life could enjoy these public areas. They could not only enjoy their tea, but they were entertained as well, usually by concerts and/or games. The idea of the tea gardens worked its way into homes. The hostess would often serve the tea in a silver heated teapot and pour the tea into the finest porcelain from China. The food served with the tea was delicate and delicious. Crumpets became one of the most desired sides for tea, along with small crustless sandwiches and pates.

There were two types of tea ceremonies at this time. Low tea, which is more what we would consider afternoon tea, was served in the more well to do homes. This was more of a 'snack' type affair than an actual meal. High tea, on the other hand, was observed by the middle and lower classes and was served as the main meal of the day with regular meat and vegetables and tea. Afternoon teas had become quite fashionable when Anna, the seventh Duchess of Bedford, had started to have her maid bring her a pot of tea and light refreshments to tide her over between her lunch and late dinner. She enjoyed this so much she soon started inviting her friends to join her. The idea for the afternoon tea caught on and soon other ladies wanted to do the same thing. This new fad opened up several markets of manufacturing. Companies started making beautiful dishes and fine linens. Cookbooks and instructions on how to prepare food, tea, and organizing a tea party became very popular.

Then the popularity of tea traveled across the Atlantic Ocean to America. America was first colonized by groups of Europeans. In Philadelphia, New York, and Boston, drinking tea was particularly fashionable. Tea and expensive porcelain and silver were symbols of wealth and the wealthy served the tea as elegantly as it was done in Europe. The drinking of tea became a symbol of good breeding and manners in the less affluent.

In 1767, however, the British began imposing a heavy tea tax on the Americans to help fund their military and leader presence in the New World. The exorbitant taxes on their favorite drink became oppressive and created a rebellion. As the events deteriorated, a group of men, dressed up as Indians, boarded the ships in Boston Harbor that were carrying a large cargo of tea and threw hundreds of pounds of the British tea into the harbor. The British government closed the harbor and then they started their troop buildup in the colonies and began the conflict that later became known as the War of Independence or Revolutionary War. In the meantime, to continue their favorite social activities of gathering together for 'tea', the Americans turned to alternate sources for their beverages. They began to drink more coffee than tea and some had turned to the herbal teas that the American Indians had introduced them to.

In the late 1800's upscale restaurants in both America and England began to offer tea services. They would have specialized areas in their restaurants called tearooms and tea courts. They became very popular during the Victorian Era. Afternoon tea dances became all the rage by 1910.

Then along came iced tea! At the first world's fair in St. Louis, Missouri an Englishmen, by the name of Richard Blechynden, was serving tea samples to the fair revelers but his business wasn't as brisk as he would have hoped. It was extremely hot one day and he had the brilliant idea to add ice to the tea and serve it cold. Needless to say it was a hit and iced tea was born! It has been a popular drink ever since that time.

Another invention born in the USA was credited to an American tea merchant, Thomas Sullivan, in New York. He began to package the loose tealeaves in hand sewn silk muslin bags. He shipped these bags of teas all over the world. When he delivered them to restaurants, he found that the baristas were brewing the tea while it was still in the bags, so he began marketing his tea 'bags' as a new and convenient way to brew tea without all the mess of loose tea.

Today, tea has become very popular in America as well as the rest of the world. Tearooms are opening up everywhere and tea, whether hot or iced, has become the best selling beverage in the world.

People are enjoying the benefits of drinking tea, whether it is the stronger, darker tea that is enjoyed in the mornings with breakfast, or the lighter varieties for the afternoon or evening meal. Tea has long been known for its health benefits. Not only does it refresh and add vigor to a tired spirit because of its varying levels of caffeine, but it also contains antioxidants that help the body cleanse itself of toxins. Add to the tea, various herbs, or just drink herbal tea, and a whole new set of refreshing and medicinal properties opens up. I will be going over some of these herbs and their benefits at the end of this book.

In keeping with this 'afternoon tea' theme, I would like to encourage you to experiment with different types of teas, whether they are straight teas from the various types of the tea tree (*Thea sinensis*), or are made from herbs, or a combination of the two. When you have friends over you can introduce them to your favorites and let them choose their own. In closing, 'afternoon teas' cannot only be a time of fellowship with your friends or family, but it can also be a time when you can just sit back and relax and enjoy a quiet time of meditation, worship, and peace.

"Under certain circumstances there are few hours in life more agreeable than the hour dedicated to the ceremony known as afternoon tea."
HENRY JAMES, 'THE PORTRAIT OF A LADY', 1880

-*Week 1*-

*And by the river upon the bank thereof, on this side
and on that side, shall grow all trees for meat, whose
leaf shall not fade, neither shall the fruit thereof be
consumed: it shall bring forth new fruit according to
his months, because their waters they issued out of the
sanctuary: and the fruit thereof shall be for meat, and
the leaf thereof for medicine.*
(EZEKIEL 47:12 KJV)

WHAT COMES TO MIND WHEN YOU THINK OF sitting down with a cup of tea?

In the springtime, I can imagine myself sitting at a table outdoors with the mild breezes blowing gently, vibrant blue skies overhead, and the smell of the flowers just beginning to bloom. In my hand, I hold my Bible open to my favorite passage of the day and meditate as I read and soak in the beauty around me and feel the love of God in me as he speaks quietly to my heart.

In the summer heat, I'm outside again, but this time I drink my cup of tea with sugar and ice and a wedge of lemon. I'm distracted from my Bible study as I wonder at the sights and sounds all about me. I hear the neighborhood children laughing and playing and the birds are singing and making a joyful noise as they fly throughout the trees, gathering in food for their young. A squirrel becomes braver as he scampers ever closer to me, wanting me to share part of my cookie or as the British would say 'biscuit' with him. As I sit there, I am in awe of God's creation. I see his handiwork in everything surrounding me and I am amazed.

In the fall, I savor the brisk, cooler days. The children are in school now and their giggling and playing is replaced by the sounds of the school buses as they go their way through the neighborhood. It becomes quieter after they are gone. I make myself a warm cup of tea and sit at my kitchen table. I enjoy spiced tea at this time of year with its sweet aromas of cinnamon and cloves. I have a bowl full of apples sitting on my counter waiting for me to make them into a delicious apple pie, but first, before I begin my busy day, I spend some time in prayer, read a devotional book or my Bible, and thank God for his grace and mercy. I also thank him for the gorgeous autumn colors that surround me, and for the bountiful harvest that he blessed us with this year.

In the winter, there is a soft blanket of snow outside and the snow is still coming down. I have nowhere to go, so I can sit back and enjoy the beauty of the season. I build a fire in the fireplace while the teakettle in my kitchen begins to sing. My heart feels at home when I pour my cup of tea. The cranberry scones I made earlier in the day are still warm and would be a delicious snack with my tea. I carry my tea and scones to the table beside my favorite chair that near the fireplace and I gather my Bible and notebook and settle in for some quality time with just Jesus, me, and my afternoon tea.

My Bible opens to Ezekiel 47:12, the only verse in the Bible that talks about tea. Although tea isn't mentioned specifically by name (that was a term made up later), It talks about trees that are evergreen and their leaves are good for medicine. Tea trees are indeed evergreen and it has been found that teas have many health benefits. God has made so many wonderful things to help us enjoy life. He gave us the seasons, a beautiful world, the comfort of tea, and most importantly, he gave us His Son.

*Thank you Lord for this time set apart to just to be
with you. Thank you for the seasons and the beauty of
the world around us and for your love.
In Jesus name, I pray. Amen.*

Jam Thumb Print Biscuits (Cookies)

2 cups self-rising flour
½ cup super-fine or baker's sugar (castor sugar in UK)
7 tablespoons of room-temperature butter
1 large egg (beaten)
4 tablespoon of strawberry jam (or any jam will do)
Large granular crystalized sugar (optional)

Preheat the oven to 375 degrees F. Prepare cookie sheet with parchment paper, or spray with cooking spray, or grease lightly. Combine flour and sugar in bowl. Add butter and blend with your hands or mixer until it resembles fine breadcrumbs. Add beaten egg and mix until it becomes a stiff dough. Flour your hands and roll dough into a log about 7 or 8 inches long. Wrap the dough and refrigerate until firm. Cut log of dough in 12 slices with a sharp knife. Place on prepared cookie sheet about 2 inches apart. Press a spoon or your thumb in center of the biscuit (cookie) to make an indention. Fill the hollow in the center of the biscuit (cookie) with 1 teaspoon of the jam. Sprinkle with large granular sugar before baking (optional). Bake for 10-15 minutes until golden brown. Cool on rack. Recipe makes 12 biscuits (cookies). Enjoy with your afternoon tea!

'Biscuits' are commonly eaten as a snack food with tea. They are usually made with flour or oats and sweetened with sugar or honey. They often contain chocolate, fruit, nuts, jams, or have a creamy filling. They are often hard, so some tea drinkers like to 'dunk' them in their tea to soften them before eating. The term 'Biscuit' is used more in the UK. 'Cookie' or 'Cracker' is more often used in the US. (Source: Wikipedia)

-Week 2-

Who can find a virtuous woman?
For her price is far above rubies.
PROVERBS 31:10 KJV

WHEN I WAS GROWING UP MY MOTHER WAS the center of our home. My father worked two jobs so it was left to my mother to care for the ten of us kids. Life wasn't always so easy for us back then. With so many mouths to feed, she had to make her limited food budget stretch. When I look back I now often wonder how she could make such tasty food and desserts. She didn't use pre-made mixes like we have today, but made everything from 'scratch'. Some of my favorite desserts were her apple pie made with the apples from the trees in our backyard. The apples were a little sour, but they made the best apple pies. Sometimes she'd make what she called apple roly-poly. It was made from homemade biscuit dough rolled out and filled with cinnamon, sugar, butter, and apples and rolled up and sliced like cinnamon rolls. After they were cooked, she'd make a sweet white sauce to cover them. My favorite dessert, however, was her strawberry-rhubarb pie. We kids would go into the fields around our house and gather wild strawberries. She would take these delicious berries and the diced stalks of the rhubarb that she grew in her garden and sweeten them with cinnamon, sugar, and thickener and it would be so delicious when made in her homemade crusts.

Later in the day, when she was through cleaning, cooking, and doing the laundry in her old wringer-washing machine and hanging the clothes

JESUS, ME, & AFTERNOON TEA

on the clothesline to dry, she would sit down to rest and we would share a cup of tea along with one of her desserts she had just made. Sometimes we'd play a board game, or cards, or just visit. Those visits were even more precious after I had grown and no longer lived at home.

She is no longer with us and I miss those days that I use to visit with her. She's in Heaven now and I don't doubt that she is now having her tea with Jesus and interceding for us, her children.

Now that I'm older and my own two girls are grown, I wonder what kind of memories they will have of me. Will they look back and wish that I had spent more time with them? Let us never be so busy that we can't take a break with our children, even if it's just a few minutes a day. So bring out those teacups and put the kettle on, buy some dessert or better yet, make one from 'scratch' (they'll appreciate it more) and enjoy today with them. While you are having your teatime together, share a smile, a thought, or just be yourself, and get to know your children better. The memories of what you do today will last forever.

Dear Heavenly Father, help me learn to make a little time each day to take a break in the midst of all my busyness just to reconnect with you. Sometimes the busier we are, the more we need it. Also help me to remember that my children need my attention too, even though they are grown. Let me leave them a legacy of caring, teaching them what's important, and most important of all, loving you. In Jesus name, I pray. Amen.

NOTES: _____

_____

_____

Strawberry-Rhubarb Pie

Preheat oven to 425 degrees F. Makes 1 pie.

Crust

1 nine inch deep dish pie crust
(store-bought or use your own favorite crust recipe).

Filling:

2 ½ cups of chopped fresh red rhubarb
(warning: use stalks only! The leaves are poisonous!)

2 ½ cups of washed, de-stemmed, and chopped strawberries

1 ½ cups sugar

2 tablespoons minute tapioca

1 tablespoon all-purpose flour

½ teaspoon lemon zest

1 teaspoon lemon juice

½ teaspoon ground cinnamon

1 teaspoon vanilla extract

3 tablespoons of butter, cubed small.

Optional: for crust coating

1 egg white beaten with 1 teaspoon of water

Large granule sugar

Mix fruit, spices, sugar, tapioca and flour together in a large bowl and pour into the piecrust. Dot the top of the filling evenly with the cubes of butter.

Brush the rim of the bottom crust with egg white mixture to help the top crust adhere better. Cover the fruit mixture with the top crust and cut small slits in the crust (a lattice crust is also very pretty with this pie).

For a shiny golden crust, brush the top crust with the egg wash mixture and sprinkle with the coarse granular sugar (optional).

Put foil around edges of pie. Bake at 425 degrees F. for 15 minutes. Decrease temperature to 375 degrees F. and bake for 45-50 minutes longer, or until the filling begins to bubble. Allow to cool before serving. Enjoy!

-*Week 3*-

And he said unto them, come ye yourselves apart into a desert place, and rest a while: for there were many coming and going, and they had no leisure so much as to eat.

MARK 6:31 KJV

H AVE YOU EVER BEEN SO BUSY YOU FORGOT to eat, never mind, stopping to take a breath and relax? Forget about setting aside time to pray and meditate on the word of God. I don't know about you, but I get that way sometimes. It was even worse when I had to go to work at my job. It was always the boss telling me: 'I need this done or that done and I don't need it later, I need it now! Stop working on that project, this is more important.' On and on it goes. Even when we don't have an outside job to go to, we glance around our house and see the dirty, sticky floors, the dust is piling up because we haven't dusted in a while. The laundry, if it's not lying around the house in need of cleaning, it's in the washer or dryer and needs to be folded or ironed and the kids are fussy and need atten-tion. Then I look at the clock... 'Oh my, hubby will be coming home soon and I don't even know what to cook for supper', and my child's (insert activity here) is tonight. By the time it's time for bed, I'm so exhausted, I can't even see straight, let alone pray and worship my God.

When you are so busy that you don't feel like you have time for God or yourself then you are too busy! Sometimes the best thing to do is sched-ule a God and you time. It is the most important part of the day. You may need to set the alarm 15 minutes earlier to meet him in the morning or write in a devotion time on your calendar and stick to it. During your devotion time, make it a celebration or a mini vacation. Afternoon teas are a perfect time to relax. Treat yourself to a warm soothing cup of tea and light refreshments. You can make it a party with others or just get away from it all and find yourself a quiet corner. Pull out your favorite devotional book or your Bible. Even if you just read one verse a day, find one that's meaningful for you and meditate on it.

Give yourself permission to take this break. Even Jesus, during his ministry took time to go off by himself to pray and he encouraged his disciples to do the same thing.

When Martha, the sister of Mary, was busy about preparing her home and meals for Jesus, Mary was sitting at his feet. Martha fussed because Mary wasn't helping and Jesus told her that Mary chose the better thing.

So give yourself permission to pour a cup of tea and take a little time for yourself. You need it. You deserve it.

Lord, please help me learn to number my days as well as my minutes and hours. Help me never to be so busy that I ignore my time with you or my family. Help me to use my time wisely. You have given everyone the same number of hours a day. Help me learn to take even a little of that time for myself so I can meditate on your word. In Jesus name, I pray. Amen.

NOTES: _____

_____

_____

"There is something in the nature of tea that leads us into a world of quiet contemplation of life."
LIN YUTANG. 'THE IMPORTANCE OF LIVING"

Cream Puffs

Filling:

2 (3.5 ounce) packages of instant vanilla pudding
(Chocolate or lemon pudding would also be great!)

2 cups heavy (whipping) cream

1 cup of milk

Pastry:

½ cup of butter

1 cup of water

¼ teaspoon of salt

1 cup of all-purpose flour

4 large eggs

Topping: (optional)

Melted chocolate chips or

Powdered sugar

Beat together the filling ingredients with a mixer or food processor. Cover and refrigerate until set and ready to use.

For the pastry: Preheat oven to 425 degrees F. In a large pot, bring water and butter to a full rolling boil. Stir in flour and salt until it forms a ball. Transfer dough to a large bowl and add eggs one at a time beating well after each addition. Drop by tablespoonfuls to an ungreased cookie sheet. Bake for 20-25 minutes or until golden brown. After they are cooled, split them and fill them with the vanilla (or other flavored) filling or pipe filling into the center with a pastry bag and nozzle tip.

If desired, you can melt chocolate chips in the microwave and drizzle over the tops (see picture), or sift some powdered sugar on top.

-*Week 4*-

Come unto me, all ye that labour and are heavy laden,
and I will give you rest. Take my yoke upon you, and
learn of me: for I am meek and lowly in heart: and ye
shall find rest unto your souls. For my yoke is easy and
my burden is light.

MATTHEW 11:28-30 KJV

IN GENESIS, AFTER THE FALL OF MAN, GOD condemned Adam and Eve to a life of burdens. Their life would no longer be the joyful, luxuriant life they had in the Garden of Eden. By disobeying God they would now have to go out and fend for themselves. They would have to plant and sow their food through the dry heat of the day. The desert wouldn't give up her crops easily. They had to work and work hard for everything they hoped to accomplish. Because of the scarcity of food, they became hunters and gatherers.

Because we are all descendants from the first man and woman, we too are born into sin. As humans, it is our bent to always take the easy way out or to step on others or cheat to succeed. It is in our nature to want the next new thing no matter what it costs us or someone else.

What does it mean to you to take on the yoke of Jesus? To me, it means that I don't have to bear the weight of my sinful nature anymore. Do I still have to work and make money so I can pay my bills? Of course I do. I don't believe that he is saying that I no longer have a responsibility to care for and provide for my family just because I become his child. That would just be absurd and totally irresponsible.

I believe what he is saying is that we will no longer be burdened by our sins. He died for our sins on the cross and he is saying that when we sin, we need to acknowledge that we need him, and let him into our hearts. The burden that we feel over all the sins in our lives is lifted at that moment of surrender. Does that mean that we are free to commit the same sins over and over again and he gives us a free pass every time? Again, I don't believe that either. If we are truly repentant we no longer have the desire to continue in that sin. God is love and if we accept that and what Christ did on the cross for us then we have the freedom to love and forgive others as he has loved and forgiven us and gave to us eternal life. Once we know that, our hearts are lighter and our burdens are easier to bear because we have a hope for the future.

Lord, Thank you for allowing me to come to you and rest in your love and forgiveness. Take away my bent of sinning and help me to love and forgive others. Give me peace and comfort as I read your word and give me courage to share it with others who need you as much as I do. In Jesus name, I pray. Amen.

NOTES: _____

_____

_____

"Strange how a teapot can represent at the same time the comforts of solitude and the pleasures of company."
AUTHOR UNKNOWN

Blueberry Scones

Preheat oven to 375 degrees F.

2 cups all-purpose flour
¼ cup packed brown sugar
1 tablespoon baking powder
¼ teaspoon salt
¼ cup butter, chilled
1 cup of rinsed and de-stemmed fresh blueberries
¾ cup half and half cream
1 large egg

Combine all the dry ingredients in large bowl. Cut in butter, either with your hands or mixer until it is the consistency of fine breadcrumbs. Add blueberries and toss to mix. In another bowl, mix egg and cream, beating well until blended thoroughly. Pour slowly and fold into the dry ingredients and berries until stiff dough forms. Knead 3-4 times. Don't overdo this or scone will be too dense. Divide dough in half and turn out each half on a flour surface. Shape each half into a six-inch disc. Cut each disc of dough into 6 equal wedges. Separate the wedges. Bake on an ungreased or parchment lined cookie sheet 1-2 inches apart for about 20 minutes at 375 degrees F. Best when served warm and fresh with a with a dollop of cream or butter and a steamy cup of tea!

For a variation of this scone, try making it with cranberries, chopped strawberries or raisins in place of the blueberries.

-*Week 5*-

For this cause, I bow my knees unto the Father of our Lord Jesus Christ, of whom the whole family in heaven and earth is named, that he would grant you, according to the riches of his glory, to be strengthened with might by his Spirit in the inner man; that Christ may dwell in your hearts by faith; that ye being rooted and grounded in love, may be able to comprehend with all saints what is the breath, and length, and depth, and height; and to know the love of Christ, which passes knowledge, that ye might be filled with all the fullness of God.

EPHESIANS 3:14-19.

'HE LOVES ME, HE LOVES ME NOT...' How many of us, as children, would gently pluck off the pedals of flowers (usually those of the daisy family) to find out if our current 'crush' loved us. It was a simple, mind-less game we played as we destroyed the beauty of the flowers in our hands to get our answer to our heart's desire and if it didn't give us the answer we hoped for, we'd simply get another one and start the process over. 'He loves me, he loves me not...' again the wrong answer? Let's try it again. Pretty soon we'd have a bouquet of the yellow centers of the once beautiful flowers and our hearts would either be shattered or elated.

It is so nice to know that we don't have to play childish games to learn whether or not Jesus loves us. All we have to do is read his words and look at the cross and trust in him.

"Greater love hath no man than this, that a man lay down his life for his friends. Ye are my friends, if ye do whatsoever I command you." John 15:13-14

Thank you Lord for the assurance that you will always love us, even though we aren't always worthy of that love. Thank you for being there for us. In Jesus name, I pray. Amen.

NOTES: _____

_____

_____

English Crumpets

Crumpets with your afternoon tea, what a treat! Gives you a feeling of a proper 'Olde' England tea! Serve them warm with butter, jam or syrup.

2 cups of all-purpose flour
2 tablespoons all-purpose flour
2 teaspoons quick-rise instant yeast
1 teaspoon of sugar
½ teaspoon of salt
1 ¼ cups of lukewarm water
1 ¼ cups of lukewarm milk
4 3-inch metal cookie cutters with open tops or crumpet molds (try fun shape cookie cutters like hearts, etc.)
Cooking spray

Whisk 2 cups plus 2 tablespoons flour, yeast, sugar and salt in a large mixing bowl. Combine the milk and water in another bowl and pour into the dry mixture and stir until the batter is thick and smooth. Cover for about an hour in a warm draft-free place and let rise until mixture is spongy. Stir the dough to reduce the sponginess. Spray skillet and cookie cutter (or molds) with cooking spray. Heat skillet and molds over medium-low heat. Spoon the batter into the molds until they are half-full. Let them cook until the tops are nearly dried and the bubbles are popped. This takes about 5 minutes. Remove molds with tongs and flip the crumpets to brown the other side, another 1-2 minutes. Rewarm them as needed before serving. Serve with butter, jam, honey, or syrup.

-Week 6-

*The LORD is my shepherd; I shall not want. He maketh
me to lie down in green pastures: he leadeth me beside
the still waters. He restoreth my soul: he leadeth me
in the paths of righteousness for his name's sake. Yea,
though I walk through the valley of the shadow of death,
I will fear no evil: for thou art with me; thy rod and thy
staff they comfort me. Thou preparest a table before me
in the presence of mine enemies: thou annointest my
head with oil; my cup runneth over. Surely goodness
and mercy shall follow me all the days of my life: and I
will dwell in the house of the LORD forever.*

PSALMS 23: 1-6

WHAT A BEAUTIFUL PICTURE OF OUR HEAVENLY FATHER. David who was a poor lowly shepherd before becoming a king wrote this wonderful psalm, one of most memorized and quoted scriptures in the Bible. It was almost prophetic in its wording. Later Jesus refers to himself as the 'Good Shepherd'. So was David looking forward to the Christ or was Jesus recalling the words of David?

As you read the psalm, imagine yourself in the place of the lamb and being led by Jesus, the Good Shepherd. Close your eyes and visualize the place where you are. There are mountains off in the distance and there is a dark, dense forest nearby, but for now you are in a lush, grassy field. Jesus is leading you beside the still waters of a stream nearby where you can stop to take a drink whenever you are thirsty. When you are tired, he allows you to rest and lie down in the soft, cool grass. He knows you need to rest your weary body and refresh your spirit. He knows that there will be rough times ahead and you will need all your strength to overcome them. However, even through the tough times, you are not alone. He will help you through the troubling times by using his rod and staff, 'the Word of God'. It is able to direct your path and bring you back to him when you, like the sheep, are led astray. His words give you comfort because you know that he will take care of you even when your enemy, the prince of darkness, threatens to destroy you. When you pass through the forest of dark and troubling times and have reached the other side of the forest of doubts, concerns, sadness and other terrible events in your life, you come to a larger and more beautiful, open field. It is bright and wondrous and full of glorious light. A table is set in the middle of this land and there are riches in store for everyone who enters into the feast. The darkness is behind you now and the enemy rages as he looks on in anger, because he can no longer get to you. When upon entering this beautiful place, the Good Shepherd anoints your head with fragrant oil and places a radiant crown on your brow. He then gives you a cup and fills it to overflowing with his mercy, grace, and love.

Oh wondrous Shepherd, give us now this moment of refreshing as we pause to take a break to study your word and fill our hearts with joy in knowing that you are there to fill our cups with love, grace and mercy. In Jesus name, I pray. Amen.

NOTES: _____

_____

_____

Cream Cheese Banana Nut Muffins

¾ cup butter, softened

8 ounces cream cheese, softened

2 cups sugar

2 large eggs

3 cups all-purpose flour

½ teaspoon baking powder

½ teaspoon baking soda

½ teaspoon salt

1 and ½ cups ripe mashed bananas (about 4 medium)

1 cup chopped walnuts or pecans

½ teaspoon vanilla extract

Preheat oven to 350 degrees F. Beat butter and cream cheese with mixer on medium until creamy. Gradually add sugar until light and fluffy. Add eggs one at a time, beating after each, until blended. Combine dry ingredients in another bowl. Add gradually to cream cheese/butter mixture, beating until blended. Mix in bananas and vanilla until consistent throughout dough. Fold in chopped nuts.

Prepare muffin tins by spraying with cooking spray or line them with muffin/cupcake liners. Fill cups 2/3 full. Bake at 350 degrees F. for 20-25 minutes or until tops are lightly brown. Cool on rack. Enjoy!

These are really good warm or cool. If you want to add some more awesome flavor to these, try adding chocolate chips, blueberries or chopped strawberries at the same time you add in the nuts!

-Week 7-

Be careful for nothing; but in every thing by prayer and supplication with thanksgiving let your requests be made known unto God, and the peace of God, which passes all understanding, shall keep your hearts and minds through Christ Jesus. Finally, brethren, whatsoever things are true, whatsoever things are honest, whatsoever things are just, whatsoever things are lovely, whatsoever things are of good report; if there be any virtue, and if there be any praise, think on these things.

PHILIPPIANS 4: 6-8

WHAT HAPPENS WHEN YOU PRAY FOR SOMETHING? Do you pray with a defeatist attitude? Do you think that God can't possibly bless you, because you haven't done anything worthy of his blessing, so why even ask? On the other hand, maybe if you are good, you think surely he will reward you with the answer 'yes' to all your requests. Maybe if you're really good and you do a lot of good works, he will give you everything your heart desires. I mean, God should reward you, right? After all, look at everything you've done for him! He owes you! Then you get downright dejected and belligerent and start spouting that you have been short-changed or even start telling everyone that God isn't real or that he never listens to you if you don't get what you want. Then you quit doing things that you thought he wanted you to do, like going to church, or praying, or giving of yourself to help others. You go sulk in your room and cry into your pillow and contend that life just isn't fair. Wait up...

God doesn't need you to work for your blessings. He doesn't expect you to throw the garbage of your good deeds at his feet. What he does expect from you is a humble heart that loves him. In Micah 6:8 it says: *'He has shown thee, O man, what is good; and what does the LORD require of thee, but to do justly, and to love mercy, and to walk humbly with thy God'.*

God has made you in his image and his ways are the right ways. If he doesn't answer right away or the answer is 'no' or 'not now', then don't get discouraged because he knows your future better than you. Maybe he says 'no' because he has something better for you, something that you aren't even aware of yet. Even when the answer is 'no', keep praying anyway. Continue to have faith and trust the Lord, as he knows what's in the future, and then thank him, even if he says 'no' to what you think you want, and above all... stay positive.

> *Dear Lord, It's so hard for me to stay positive at times, especially when I see so many things happening in the world that appear to be against everything I believe in, everything I love. Lord, you know the end of all things. You know our future and you know what's best for us. Give us courage and instill in us a faith that everything will work out in our lives for your glory because we love you and our hearts can safely trust in you. In Jesus name, I pray. Amen.*

NOTES: _____

_____

_____

"A cup of tea is a cup of peace."
SOSHITSU SEN XV

Gingerbread Tea Cake

½ cup sugar

½ cup of butter or margarine

1 large egg

1 cup molasses

2 ½ cups all-purpose flour

1 ½ teaspoons baking soda

1 teaspoon ground cinnamon

1 teaspoon ground ginger

½ teaspoon ground cloves

½ teaspoon salt

1 cup hot water or tea

Preheat oven to 350 degrees F. Spray a 9 inch square pan with cooking spray or grease and flour. In a large bowl, cream the sugar and butter (or margarine) until light and fluffy, beat in the egg and then the molasses. In another bowl, blend the flour, baking soda, salt, and the spices. Blend into the creamed butter mixture. Stir in the hot water. Pour into the pan. Bake 1 hour in the preheated oven until a knife inserted in the middle comes out clean. Cool in pan. Frost as desired or sprinkle with confectionary sugar. This cream cheese frosting would be delicious on this:

Cream cheese icing:

½ cup butter (room temperature)

8 oz. of cream cheese (room temperature)

2-3 cups of powdered sugar

1 teaspoon vanilla extract

With an electric mixer, blend the butter and cream cheese together on medium speed. Add the vanilla and mix in. Slowly add in the powdered sugar and mix until smooth. Spread on cake. Add more powdered sugar if needed to get the right consistency.

-*Week 8*-

...A certain man made a great supper, and bade many: and sent his servant at suppertime to say to them that were bidden, 'Come; for all things are now ready.' And they all with one consent began to make excuse...

LUKE 14:16B-18A

And the servant said, 'Lord, it is done as thou hast commanded, and yet there is room.' And the lord said unto the servant, 'Go out into the highways and hedges, and compel them to come in, that my house may be filled.'

LUKE 14:22-23

IT WAS GOING TO BE THE MOST WONDERFUL afternoon tea ever in your history of having tea parties. You've spent weeks working on the party favors and looking up the most delicious and traditional recipes for canapés, sandwiches, and teacakes. You even went to the most expensive tea-shops to find the perfect teas. You had to go out of your way to search for the more exotic ingredients for your recipes that your local grocery store didn't carry. You spent a fortune, but you didn't mind. After all, your friends were worth it.

The excitement was building because the day was drawing closer. You would spend the better part of the day before the party, decorating and pulling out your beautiful silver tea set. It was tarnished and you had to polish it because it hadn't been used in a while. You admired your expensive beautiful new china you had just bought for the party and thought how envious everyone would be because of your wonderful taste. No one would ever be able to top this! The morning of the day of the party, you worked yourself up into a frenzy, preparing all of the food. You knew that once the guests arrived, the exhaustion from all the hard work would ease and everyone would have a fantastic time and would fawn over everything you had done.

When everything was finished you sat down to call everyone to remind them of what time they should be there. They had all been sent the beautiful invitations that you had carefully created using lace and ribbons. All your friends had replied that they would most certainly be there. Even though you hadn't talked with them in a day or two, you didn't worry because you all were so close. You knew they wouldn't let you down, but as you talked with each of them, they started making excuses. One said it had completely slipped her mind and she had made an appointment with her hairdresser. Another had to pick up her child from soccer practice at that time. Another said that she had started on a diet. On and on, everyone had excuses. They promised that another day would be better and they most certainly would come the next time you had a party.

Bruised and dejected, you started to clear away the food when a thought came to mind. You remembered the story in Luke, chapter 14. It was the parable that Jesus told about the man who was going to have a feast and then nobody showed up. It was a parable he told about God's mercy. It was free for anyone who was invited to partake of it, but when they refused or made excuses, he went to others who would gladly receive it. So you dusted off your disappointment and set aside your sadness, then you began to smile as you thought, 'God gave me much to be thankful for, so I'm going to share what he gave to me with others who would love to have to have a special afternoon tea.' So with that thought in mind, you called the homeless women's center in town and ask them if their patrons would be interested in a tea party.

Thank you Lord for all you have given to me. Show me ways that I can use those blessings to help others. In Jesus name, I pray. Amen.

Easy Petits Fours

1 16 ounce frozen pound cake (e.g. Sara Lee)
1 jar raspberry or strawberry jam
2 cans vanilla frosting
Food color paste (your choice of colors, do not use liquid food color)
Sprinkles or sugar pearls or other decorations (optional)

Using a sharp knife, slice the pound cake horizontally in 3 layers. Spread the jam over the bottom two layers and put the top layer over the two layers. Cut the cake in one-inch squares. Heat one can of frosting in the microwave for 15-20 seconds until it's the consistency of heavy cream (or you can make your own frosting). Stir in a small amount of food coloring until you get the color you want. Holding the cake square above a cookie sheet or bowl (using a fork to hold it up works well) drizzle the frosting over the entire square to completely cover it. Place on a drying rack and decorate with your choice of decorations. It is done when the frosting is hardened and dry. Store in refrigerator until ready to serve. For a decorative touch, set each in a fancy mini-cupcake/muffin liner.

For fun, make a few extra and put them in a decorative box as a take home gift for your guests. Wonderful gift idea for Easter or Christmas! Experiment with different types of pound cakes and fillings (lemon, strawberry or chocolate would be delicious).

A petit four is a small confectionary appetizer. The name is French meaning "small oven".

-Week 9-

But the fruit of the Spirit is love, joy, peace, longsuffering,
gentleness, goodness, faith, meekness, temperance:
against such there is no law.
GALATIANS 5:22-23 KJV

WALKING THROUGH THE CHRISTIAN BOOKSTORE THE OTHER DAY, my eyes caught a glimpse of several plaques and paintings on the wall. They ranged from colorful to rustic. There were paintings of beautiful flowers, birds, and butterflies, or still lifes of fruit and flowers. There were even a few hand- carved wooden plaques. Each of them had the words 'Fruits of the Spirit' or a single word: 'Love, Joy, Peace, Longsuffering, Gentleness, Goodness, Faith, Meekness, or Temperance'. Just looking at the words on that wall and taking in their meanings, helped me to relax. Such beautiful words and pictures, how could anyone choose one of the paintings over another? What fruit would be the one I would choose, if I could only have one? How wonderful it would be, to be fully blessed with all of them.

As I was making my decision, I thought of the definitions of each:
- **Love:** A feeling of warm personal attachment or affection toward another person.
- **Joy:** A feeling of great pleasure and happiness.
- **Peace:** An occurrence of harmony characterized by the lack of violence, conflicting behaviors, and the freedom from fear of violence.

- **Longsuffering:** Patiently enduring wrongs or difficulties.
- **Gentleness:** Considerate or kindly in disposition, amiable and tender.
- **Goodness:** The state or quality of being good. Moral excellence or virtue.
- **Faith:** Confidence or trust in a person, thing, deity or in the teachings of a religion or view.
- **Meekness:** Humbly patient or docile, as under provocation from others.
- **Temperance:** moderation or self-restraint in actions or statements. Self control.

As I looked over the wall, I finally found a beautiful painting that quoted the whole verse found in Galatians 5:22-23. I gleefully found the box, took it to the cashier and walked out with my prize. It is now on my wall, but I know that it isn't enough to admire it as a piece of art, but I need to live it in my heart.

Dear Heavenly Father, help me realize it's not enough to memorize your word and admire some of them on a painting, but I need to infuse them into my heart and soul. As a vulnerable, sinful human, it's often hard to live up to the words in these verses, but until I do, I cannot know my true potential I have as your child, overflowing in my harvest of the fruits of the spirit. In Jesus name, I pray. Amen.

NOTES: _____

_____

_____

"You can never get a cup of tea large enough or a book long enough to suit me."
C.S. LEWIS

Fresh Fruit Tartlets

1 envelope of whipped topping mix (e.g. Dream Whip)

½ cup cold milk

1 teaspoon vanilla extract

1 8 oz. package of cream cheese (softened)

½ cup of confectioners' sugar

Individual tart shells (you can either use graham-cracker shells or frozen pastry shells (follow directions on how to bake)

Fresh fruit of your choice

Garnish as desired with edible flowers or mint leaves (optional)

Bake tart shells in oven and allow to cool (if using frozen pastry shells).

In a small bowl beat the topping mix, milk, and vanilla on low speed until blended then increase to high speed until the mixture is the consistency of whipped cream. In another larger bowl, beat cream cheese and confectioner's sugar until smooth. Fold into the whipped topping.

Spoon into cooled tart shells and top with fruit. Refrigerate tartlets and left over filling. Makes 10 larger tartlets or up to 24 small ones depending on the size of the shells.

These make beautiful and colorful appetizers. Choices of fruit could include: blueberries, sliced strawberries, mandarin oranges, kiwifruit, bananas, or pineapple, or why not a combination of these? They would be perfect at your next afternoon tea.

-Week 10-

It is of the LORD's mercies that we are not consumed,
because his compassions fail not. They are new every
morning: great is thy faithfulness. The LORD is my
portion, saith my soul; therefore will I hope in him.

LAMENTATIONS 3:22-24

FROM THE MOMENT YOU WOKE UP THIS MORNING, it started… You had an interview for your dream job and you were excited. The prospects looked good for you to actually get this one. After being out of work for several months, you were looking forward to finally being able to buy groceries and paying your bills. Then it began. Your alarm didn't go off because you forgot to set it, so you only had a half hour to get ready and drive across town. No time for breakfast or even a cup of tea, you rushed to your closet to pull out your favorite suit you liked to wear to interviews, and you found that it was wrinkled. You wore it anyway, thinking that maybe it would smooth out as you wore it in the hot car. You didn't have time to style your hair, so you ran a comb through it and fluffed it up and then slapped on some lipstick and rouge. No time for the whole make-up thing. The only pair of hose you owned had runners in them. Oh well, forget the hose, go barelegged, 'no one will know the difference', you told yourself. Then when you got out your shoes, you noticed that they were dirty and scuffed. Great, you were running late and you were thinking that the person interviewing you would never give you a job, looking like a slob and not even being on time. You quickly grabbed your purse only to find that it wasn't closed and all of your things from the handbag scattered all over the kitchen floor. You quickly picked up everything and ran out the door and locked it. You jumped in your car and that's when you realized that you didn't have your resume, so you opened your bag to get out your keys so you could run back in the house to get it. That's when you realized that you didn't have your keys! Thankfully, you remembered that there is a spare house key under the doormat. You quickly found your keys and resume and headed back out to the car. You were already annoyed with the rough morning you have had, and now it didn't help that the traffic was slow because there had been a wreck on the highway.

Suddenly your cell phone rang. It was the receptionist at the office where your interview was to take place. She was calling to remind you about your interview scheduled for ...tomorrow! You started laughing hysterically as the person in the car beside you wondered what was wrong with you. At that moment you made the decision to pull off the highway at the next exit. You were suddenly very hungry and decided to pull into this cute little teashop to get some breakfast. The variety of cookies and pastries looked delicious and as you placed your order, an old adage came into your mind: 'When life give's you lemons, make lemonade' or in this case 'lemon bars'.

Later in the day, as you thought about the events of the morning, you had to smile. You thanked God that even when things go wrong, there is always a reason to praise him.

Thank you Father for all the events, whether they are good or bad, in our lives. If we are living according to your will then you will direct our steps where they are to lead us. Help us to make the moments of our lives memorable, and our actions honorable to you. In Jesus name, I pray. Amen.

NOTES: _____

_____

_____

Lemon Bars

Crust

1cup butter, softened

½ cup white sugar

2 cups all-purpose flour

Filling

4 eggs

1 ½ cups white sugar

¼ cup flour

2 lemons, juiced (about 2 tablespoons)

Optional: Confectionary sugar

Preheat oven to 350 degrees F. In a medium bowl blend together the 2 cups of flour, butter and ½ cup sugar. Press into the bottom of an ungreased 9X13 pan. Bake for 15-20 minutes until firm and lightly brown. In another bowl, mix 1 and ½ cups of sugar and ¼ cup flour. Whisk in the 4 eggs and lemon juice. Pour over the baked crust. Bake for an additional 20 minutes. The bars will become firm as they cool.

Optional: Sprinkle lightly with Confectionary Sugar.

For a variation of this recipe: Replace the lemons with limes and a drop of green food coloring for pretty lime bars!

-Week 11-

Blessed is the man that walketh not in the counsel of the ungodly, nor standeth in the way of sinners, nor sitteth in the seat of the scornful. But his delight is in the law of the LORD; and in his law doth he meditate day and night. And he shall be like a tree planted by the rivers of water that bringeth forth his fruit in his season; his leaf also shall not wither; and whatsoever he doeth shall prosper.

PSALMS 1:1-3

RANDI LOVED TO GET UP EARLY IN THE morning with her cup of tea in one hand and her Bible in the other. It was her favorite part of the day. Sometimes she would even go out on the deck when it was nice and enjoy watching the sunrise as she meditated on the beauty of God's world. This was her time. The time she spent in quietness and solitude with her Lord. All too soon she would have to put her Bible away and don her clothes to get ready to go to work, or as she would like to say 'the real world'. She would continue to mediate on the verse she found that day as she was on her commute to work. She liked to memorize the verses she had learned so she would have them fresh in her mind when someone would ask her what her reason was for her hope in God, but sadly no one at work ever did. There were so many meetings she had to attend at work: a planning meeting in the morning, a budget meeting in the afternoon, and endless meetings with clients the rest of the day. It was a struggle to not get swept into the moment when her boss or fellow workers began to gossip, tell off-color jokes, or occasionally use God's name in vain. The very hairs on her neck would stand straight up and she would blush as she continued to listen to everyone's daily diatribe against someone who wasn't present or one of their clients. She wanted to excuse herself from the meeting rather than be part of their scornful ways. One day, they noticed that she was sitting quietly with her eyes closed and her lips moving. Surely they thought that she was ignoring them or mumbling something under her breath about them, but she was quoting to herself, 1 Peter 3:15-16: *"But sanctify the Lord God in your hearts: and be ready always to give an answer to every man that asks you a reason of the hope that is in you with meekness and fear..."*

Because she was a Christian, she knew that even though she was part of this world, she was set apart. She was a child of God and she knew, if asked, she would always be ready to give an answer for her salvation. Later in the day, one of her workmates sat down to eat with her. While lingering after finishing their lunch, they began to talk about the meetings. Her co-worker asked her why she never participated in the crude conversations. She told her about her salvation and how she use to be just like them, but now that she was saved, she found the discussions around the table rude and insensitive. Her new friend said she'd like to learn more about this Jesus and what it meant to be saved. Later that afternoon, she met with her over a cup of tea in Randi's office. She shared the plan of salvation with her and her co-worker became her new friend and sister in the Lord. From that time on they both looked forward to getting together everyday with their daily afternoon teas with Jesus.

Thank you Lord that we can always find a time and place to get away from the 'world'. Help us to always find a way to share your word with those around us. In Jesus name, I pray. Amen.

NOTES: _____

_____

_____

Swedish Tea Cakes

1 cup butter, softened

½ cup confectionary sugar

2 teaspoons vanilla extract

2 ¼ cups all-purpose flour

¼ teaspoon salt

¾ cups finely chopped toasted nuts of your choice

Powdered sugar

Toast nuts on baking sheet in a 400 degree F. oven for 7-10 minutes.

In a large bowl, cream butter, ½ cup powdered sugar, and vanilla until light and fluffy. Add flour and salt mixture beating until well mixed. Mix in nuts. Cover dough and refrigerate at least 1 hour or more. Preheat oven to 400 degrees F. Roll dough into 1 inch balls. Place dough on ungreased cookie sheet 1 inch apart. Bake for 10-12 minutes until set (do not brown). Cool slightly. While the cookies are still warm roll them in powdered sugar until coated. After they are cool, roll them again in the powdered sugar (the first coating melts into the cookie and the second gives them the nice powdery coating).

These pretty little cookies are beautiful for Christmas or weddings.

"My hour for tea is half-past five, and my buttered toast waits for nobody."

WILKIE COLLINS, THE WOMAN IN WHITE

-Week 12-

And why take ye thought for raiment? Consider the lilies of the field, how they grow; they toil not, neither do they spin, and yet I say unto you that even Solomon in all his glory was not arrayed like one of these. Wherefore, if God so clothe the grass of the field, which today is and tomorrow is cast into the oven, shall he not much more clothe you, O ye of little faith? Therefore take no thought, saying, what shall we eat or what shall we drink or wherewithal shall we be clothed? For after all these things do the Gentiles seek, for your heavenly Father knows that ye have need of all these things. But seek ye first the kingdom of God and his righteousness, and all these things shall be added unto you.

MATTHEW 6:28-33

EVERYONE WOULD HAVE TO AGREE THAT FLOWERS ARE beautiful. It is like God's signature on his creation. No matter how tiny the smallest flower is, or how showy is the largest flower, they are a miracle of creation. I majored in biology when I was working on my master's degree and I even had the opportunity to do some illustrations for some biology books (my plan was to be a biological illustrator back in the day). I was privileged to dissect some flowers and look at their various parts under a microscope to illustrate their smallest details. It never ceased to amaze me how a tiny non-descript seed could be planted in the soil, later emerge and grow, first with its roots and leaves, then the buds, and at last into a full blooming flower. Even in its death, its seeds develop to be planted again to start the cycle all over again. When looking through a microscope it is truly amazing to see the tiny veins that bring nourishment to every cell of the plant so that it can create its own food to grow, and give off oxygen from its leaves through the process of photosynthesis so that we can breath fresh purified air. Speaking of breathing, what a lovely fragrance each flower has. God knew that each flower would have to emit its own peculiar fragrance to attract insects and butterflies so that the pollen (another miracle of creation) could be transferred from one flower to the next, assuring that the new seeds could grow properly.

How can anyone, after seeing the wide universe and then centering their vision through the microscope at the smallest creations, ever deny the existence of God? How can we ever worry that the God that created all of this won't take care of us, his most prized creation?

Dear Heavenly Father, thank you for your beautiful world. Help me learn to take the time to enjoy your creation, from the beautiful sky with all its glories to the smallest flowers. Help me not to worry about what I'm going to wear or eat and drink because I know you love me and will take care of me. In Jesus name I pray. Amen.

NOTES: _____

_____

_____

"If you are cold, tea will warm you;
If you are too heated, it will cool you;
If you are depressed, it will cheer you;
If you are excited, it will calm you."
WILLIAM EWART GLADSTONE

53

Pumpkin Tea Cake

1 (15 ounce) can of solid-packed pumpkin puree

1 cup of vegetable oil

4 extra large eggs

2 cups granulated sugar

2 cups of flour

1 teaspoon baking soda

1 teaspoon baking powder

2 teaspoons ground cinnamon

½ teaspoon salt

1 teaspoon vanilla

¼ cup finely chopped walnuts or pecans (optional)

Powdered sugar (optional)

Whipped cream or Frosting (optional)

Preheat oven to 350 degrees F. Grease and flour (or use cooking spray) a Bundt pan or 9X13 cake pan. Beat together the pumpkin puree, oil, eggs, and sugar. Set aside. In a separate bowl, blend together flour, baking soda, baking powder, cinnamon, and salt and add to mixture along with the vanilla extract and beat until evenly mixed together. Stir in chopped nuts. Pour mixture into prepared cake pan. Sprinkle the top with additional ground cinnamon. Bake for 30-40 minutes or until a toothpick inserted in center comes out clean. Remove from oven and allow to cool. If using a Bundt pan invert pan over a plate to allow it to gently loosen from pan. Sprinkle with powered sugar, or drizzle with a light frosting glaze or slice and serve with a dollop of whipped cream.

This would be a great dessert for your holiday teas!

-Week 13-

Not forsaking the assembling of ourselves together, as the manner of some is; but exhorting one another and so much the more, as ye see the day approaching.

HEBREWS 10:25

'THE DAYS HAVE BECOME DARKENED WITH THE SIN of mankind. Religious persecution is rampant. Churches are being closed because of lack of interest. They can no longer substantiate the reason for staying open. Satan is winning the hearts of humans and drawing together his army of fallen angels to crush what remains of the faithful Christians.'

What a horrible thought! Is this something out of the mind of those who write novels about the end times? No, this is really happening and has been prophesied throughout the Bible. As a matter of fact there have been many incidents throughout history where Satan had the upper hand and tried to crush the spirit of God's chosen people. Today, all we have to do is pick up a newspaper or look at the news on the Internet. Satan is winning the battle for men's hearts. I go to church and see so many empty pews. Just when Christians need to be on guard and assembling with other Christians, they prefer to stay home and either sleep in on Sundays or go to some church where they can be 'entertained'.

But as an individual, you can be faithful. Do not lose heart. Even if you are the only one, Christ died for your sins. Satan cannot steal your soul.

Be strong, for Christ is strong. Commit yourself to his grace and mercy. Meet with your friends. If they are Christians, study the Word together. If they are not Christians, help them. Show them what it means to be saved. Encourage one another. A perfect way to help each other is to have a daily or weekly Bible study. It doesn't have to be an elaborate affair. You don't have to have a room full of people. Even if it's just two people, get together anyway. Lift each other up in prayer, and pray for others. Soon others will come. In Ecclesiastes 4:12 it says *'and if one prevail against him, two shall withstand him; and a threefold cord is not quickly broken.'*

You may not know too many people, but you can start by finding a time of quiet rest where you can commune with God. Later on, you can tell others about your special time you have in Bible study while having an afternoon cup of tea. Invite others to share in this time. You might be surprised at just how many people there are that would love to share this time with you.

Father, help me to not be discouraged when I see everything that is going on around me. I know you are still in control even though there are battles for the hearts of mankind. Satan hasn't won yet, nor will he ever win. Help me remember that you will be victorious in the end. Thank you for my special time of Bible study. Show me ways that I can share this study with others. In Jesus name, I pray. Amen.

NOTES: _____

_____

_____

"Tea is quiet and our thirst for tea is never far from our craving for beauty."
JAMES NORWOOD PRATT

Snickerdoodles

	1 cup butter
	1 ½ cups sugar
	2 large eggs
	2 ¾ cups flour
	2 teaspoons cream of tarter
	1 teaspoon baking soda
	¼ teaspoon salt

Coating

	3 tablespoons sugar
	3 teaspoons cinnamon

Preheat oven to 350 degrees F. Mix softened butter, 1 ½ cups sugar and eggs thoroughly with mixer until light and fluffy. Combine dry ingredients in a separate bowl. Blend the dry ingredients with the butter mixture until stiff dough forms. Chill dough until firm. While chilling, mix 3 tablespoons sugar and 3 teaspoons of cinnamon in small bowl. Form 1-inch balls of chilled dough and roll them in the cinnamon mixture. Coat completely. Place on a chilled ungreased cookie sheet about 2 inches apart and bake 10 minutes. Remove from pan immediately to prevent further cooking.

Fun fact: The Joy of Cooking' cookbook claims that snickerdoodles are probably German in origin and that the name is a corruption of the German word 'Schneckennudeln' (snail noodles), a kind of pastry. Or it could be just a made up nonsense word. (Wikipedia)

-Week 14-

Ye are the light of the world. A city that is set on a hill cannot be hid, neither do men light a candle and put it under a bushel, but on a candlestick and it giveth light unto all that are in the house. Let your light so shine before men that they may see your good works, and glorify your Father who is in heaven.

MATTHEW 4:14-16

WHO DOESN'T LIKE THE AMBIANCE AND THE WARMTH of a softly flickering candle? They give a soft glow to a romantic dinner or party. When in the bathroom, they give the feeling of a relaxing spa, especially if they are gently scented and the lights are turned low. Some scented candles bring to mind our favorite flowers or pastries, like apple pies, sugar cookies, or cinnamon rolls. I even had a candle once that had the fragrance of Chi tea with its delicate spices.

Candles remind us of our favorite times: weddings, birthdays, and Christmas, most notably. I love candlelight services at Christmastime. I love how one person starts out with one lit candle in the darkened sanctuary and then as the flame is passed from one person to the next, the room gets lighter and lighter. It represents that even in the darkest world, we can be a light and spread the light to others. The unity candle at weddings demonstrates how two separate lives (candle flames) come together to form one unit (one flame). Candles on birthday cakes represent our years that we have lived on this earth. Each candle as it is blown out represents the years that are now long gone.

Candles are often lit in adjunct to worship services and prayer vigils to represent what Christ said: *"I am the light of the world"*. It is a part of prayer in some religions.

Throughout history, prior to the invention of electricity, candles and oil lamps were the only way to light up a room. In Jesus day this was their main use.

When Jesus said in Matthew, chapter 5 that 'we are to be the light of the world' he was comparing us to the flame of a candle. Without our testimony the world would remain in darkness. He also summons us to not hide our light under a bushel basket, but to shine for him and light the way so others can learn the way to salvation.

When you light the candles in your home or at church, whether in prayer, unity, marking the passing of the years, or just relaxing, remember the admonition of Jesus, to be a light in this world.

Heavenly Father, as I sit here, taking in the sweet fragrance of the candles at my table and sipping my tea, I am suddenly aware that I can no longer keep my love for you buried deep inside of me. Help me to always be a light that others will see and know that I'm a Christian and I am concerned about their salvation. In Jesus name, I pray. Amen.

NOTES: _____

_____

_____

"Water is the mother of tea, a teapot its father, and fire the teacher."
CHINESE PROVERB

Tiramisu

6 egg yolks

1 ¼ cups sugar

1 ¼ cups mascarpone cheese
(You can substitute a mixture of 8 oz. cream cheese
¼ cup heavy cream and 2 ½ tablespoons sour cream for this)

1 ¾ cups heavy whipping cream

2 (12 packages) ladyfingers

1/3 cup coffee flavored liqueur
(For a non-alcoholic version of this liqueur use 1 tsp. instant
coffee with 2 tbsp. of water and ½ to 1 teaspoon of powdered
cocoa. Add water to make 1/3 cup for recipe)

1 teaspoon unsweetened cocoa powder (for dusting)

1 (1ounce) square semisweet chocolate (optional)

Combine egg yolks and sugar in top of double boiler over boiling water. Reduce heat to low and cook for about 10 minutes stirring continually. Remove from heat and whip mixture until thick and lemon yellow colored. Add cheese to whipped yolk mixture and beat until they are fully combined. In a separate bowl, whip cream until stiff peaks form. Fold into yolk mixture. Split the ladyfingers in half and line the bottom of bowl or pan. Brush them with the coffee liqueur (or substitute). Spoon half of the creamy filling over the ladyfingers. Repeat layers starting with ladyfingers, then the coffee liqueur and finish with the rest of the creamy filling. Dust the entire surface with the unsweetened cocoa powder. To give it an extra scrumptious chocolate flavor, garnish with chocolate curls. Make chocolate curls by scrapping the edge of a semisweet chocolate bars with a vegetable peeler or grater. Sprinkle curls over top. Refrigerate several hours until set.

-*Week 15*-

He hath made everything beautiful in his time: also he hath set the world in their heart, so that no man can find out the work that God makes from the beginning to the end. I know that there is no good in them, but for a man to rejoice, and to do good in his life. And also that every man should eat and drink, and enjoy the good of all his labor; it is the gift of God.

ECCLESIASTES 3:11-13

H E WAS THE WEALTHIEST AND WISEST MAN ON the planet. He had everything and did anything he wanted. He was the king. He even built a magnificent temple to Yahweh, our God. People came from all around seeking his advice because of his wisdom, but he was not happy. I'm sure he had moments of happiness, but he always wanted more. He had seven hundred wives and 300 concubines from all over the known world. Many of them were princesses. But even after everything that God blessed him with, he was not completely happy.

The book of Ecclesiastes is a sad book. It has many beautiful passages, but it is a book of someone who at the end of his life looks back and realizes that everything he was, everything he obtained in life, and everything he accomplished wasn't ever enough.

Solomon turned away from God to worship the gods of some of his wives. He gave into the philosophy to take everything he could from life, to 'eat, drink, and be merry' and to enjoy the good of his labor. Alas, after he had done all these things he still had an emptiness in his heart. With all his wealth and wisdom, he couldn't find a way to save himself. After his death, his kingdom was divided. As a matter of fact, everything he had done was gone, except for his words of wisdom canonized in our Bible as the Proverbs, Ecclesiastes, and Song of Solomon.

Am I advocating a life of despondency and self-loathing? Of course not! I wouldn't be writing this book about enjoying afternoon teas, if that were the case, but I am encouraging everyone, not to turn away from Jesus while we are enjoying our life. God did give us a life to enjoy all of his creation. He not only wants us to be happy, but he also wants us to present our hearts to him through love and faithfulness and to show others the true way to happiness, the happiness that can only come by serving him.

Our Father in Heaven, be with us and guide us to find our true source of happiness. Help us learn that worldly things will pass, but you are forever. Teach us the way to truly enjoy the fruits of our labor, by giving you the glory for what we have. In Jesus name, I pray. Amen.

NOTES: _____

_____

_____

"There is no need to have any special attitude while drinking except one of thankfulness. The nature of the tea itself is that of no-mind."
POJONG SUNIM

Chocolate Chip Chocolate Muffins
With Walnuts

Preheat oven to 400 degrees F. Recipe makes 12 muffins

1 ¾ cups of all-purpose flour
½ cup packed brown sugar
¼ cup unsweetened cocoa powder
1 teaspoon baking powder
1 teaspoon baking soda
¼ teaspoon salt
1 cup warm water
¼ cup vegetable oil
1 tablespoon red wine vinegar
1 teaspoon vanilla extract
1 large egg, lightly beaten
½ cup semisweet chocolate mini-chips (divided)
½ cup chopped walnuts (divided)

Mix all of the dry ingredients in a large bowl, blending them thoroughly. Make a well in the center of the dry ingredients. In a smaller bowl, lightly beat the egg, then add the rest of the liquid ingredients to the egg and mix the liquids together with a whisk or fork. Pour liquid mixture into the well in the dry ingredients. Stir until just moist. Add half of the chocolate chips and walnuts to the batter, saving the rest for the topping.

Place muffin liners in muffin cups and spray liners with cooking spray. Evenly divide batter into the 12 liners. Sprinkle each with the remaining chocolate chips and walnuts. Bake at 400 degrees F. for 15 minutes or until a wooden pick inserted in center comes out clean. Cool in pan. Serve warm or cool.

-Week 16-

But he answered and said, 'It is written, Man shall not live by bread alone, but by every word that proceedeth out of the mouth of God'.

MATTHEW 4:4

IT HAD BEEN FORTY DAYS SINCE HE'D EATEN and he was weary from wandering about in the wilderness. There was no one else around him for miles. He loved people and he missed his friends and family. What would his cousin John think of him now, if he could see him? He smiled when he thought of his baptism by John and how the dove came down from Heaven and sat on his shoulder. What could the people around them be thinking when they heard the voice of God saying 'This is my beloved Son, in whom I am well pleased'. His loneliness now was almost unbearable. He would often stop to rest in the heat of the day and find shelter in the shade of a small tree or a rock. The land was dusty and barren. When he found a source of water, it was often just enough to wet his parched lips. He knew that he had to endure this time of testing and knew that this wouldn't be the last time he would suffer for mankind. On the forty-first day he saw someone coming. Was this someone bringing him news or coming to lead him home, or was he hallucinating from not having anything to eat in forty days, and only thought he saw someone? He knelt down beside a rock and prayed to his Father. He would need all of the strength he had left to survive this testing. All of a sudden he felt very hungry. The stranger pulled him to a standing position. "You see all of these stones here?" He asked. "Surely, as the Son of God, all you have to do is command these stones to be turned into bread." But he answered him with scripture, *"It is written, Man shall not live by bread alone, but by every word that proceedeth out of the mouth of God".* Then the stranger tempted him two more times. He was transported to the highest peak of the temple and the stranger told him to jump and command the angels to protect him from injury as he fell. Then he replied to the stranger, *"Thou shalt not tempt the Lord thy God."* The stranger had one more trick up his sleeve. Surely no one would say no to having the power to rule over vast lands and kingdoms. So he took the man to the top of the highest mountain, and showed him all of the kingdoms of the world. All he had to do was bow down and worship the stranger and everything he saw would be his, but the Son of God replied, *"Get thee hence, Satan: for it is written, 'Thou shalt worship the Lord thy God, and him only shalt thou serve'."* With that, the stranger left his side and with the man's strength ebbing, the heavens opened up and angels appeared to him and gave him sustenance.

> *Dear Lord, Sometimes I feel like I just can't go on and my world seems to be falling away from under my feet. Give me the power to carry on, just as you carried on in the wilderness. I know I can do all things with you as my strength. Your word says it, and I believe it. Thank you for this assurance. In Jesus name, I pray. Amen.*

NOTES: _____

_____

_____

Cream Cheese Mints

1 (3 ounce) package of cream cheese

1 tablespoon butter (softened)

3 cups confectionary sugar

2 drops peppermint oil

Food color paste

In a large bowl combine all ingredients. Make sure the butter and cream cheese is completely blended and consistent throughout. Color as desired with food color paste or leave white.

These can be made in different shapes by using candy molds. When you use molds roll a pinch of the mixture into a small ball and coat with granulated sugar. Press into the mold and pop out onto wax paper. If you don't have molds you can also roll the mixture into a small ball and press flat into a wafer with a fork that was dipped in confectioners sugar. You can also roll dough into a long thin "string/rope" and cut at ½ inch intervals (see photo). Whatever shape you make them, allow them to dry for about 2 hours on waxed paper. You can then freeze or refrigerate them until served. They can be kept in the freezer for up to 2 months.

These mints are delicious and melts in your mouth. I like to make red and green ones at Christmas time and use Christmas molds. They are also great for baby or wedding showers and tea parties, of course! Have fun with the coloring. You can color them to match a wedding or baby shower or any party theme.

-Week 17-

O GOD, thou art my God; early will I seek thee: my soul thirsteth for thee, my flesh longeth for thee in a dry and thirsty land, where no water is; to see thy power and thy glory, so as I have seen thee in the sanctuary. Because thy loving kindness is better than life, my lips shall praise thee. Thus will I bless thee while I live: I will lift up my hands in thy name. My soul shall be satisfied as with marrow and fatness; and my mouth shall praise thee with joyful lips: when I remember thee upon my bed, and meditate on thee in the night watches. Because thou hast been my help, therefore in the shadow of thy wings will I rejoice.

PSALM 63:1-7

Do you remember when you first fell in love with someone? You had them on your mind continually. They were there in your thoughts when you woke up in the morning. When you saw the sunrise, you thanked God for the beautiful new day he gave you because your heart was filled with the promise that today your love could only become more fulfilling. You could face anything now because the future seemed brighter somehow. When you were apart you were hungering and thirsting for the time you would be together again. You had trouble concentrating on your chores for the day because you were constantly daydreaming of your love. In the afternoon while you were taking your tea break you called him, just to hear his voice and make plans for your next date. As you talked, you wrote his name over and over again with doodled flowers and hearts on your notepad. After work you showered and spent hours on your clothes and makeup to make sure you looked perfect for him. Your date was wonderful as he he declared his love for you and told you he would never leave you. When you were finally able to go to sleep after your date, you dreamed of your perfect life together and your hopes for the future.

Did you feel that same way when you first fell in love with Jesus? Did you wake up, praising him and thanking him for being in your life? Did you constantly think of him throughout the day, wishing you could be even closer and more fulfilled in his love? What about your afternoon tea-time? Did you get his love letter (the Bible) off the shelf and study it, longing to learn more about him? How did you prepare yourself for meeting him in the evening hour of prayer? Did you look forward to a time of worship and praise as you settled down to rest for the night? Did you dream of the perfect future with him in Heaven and long for the day when you would be eternally with him?

What about now? Do you still feel in love with him and long for his daily presence in your life?

> *Lord, I long to feel your presence in my life. Your love is the best part of me. Help me to seek you diligently in this dry and thirsty land because I know that you love me and want what's best for me. Rekindle the love in my heart that I had when I first met you, so that I will be eager to learn more about you and have you as the center of my existence again. In Jesus name, I pray. Amen.*

NOTES: _____

_____

_____

Cheesecake Stuffed Strawberries

1 pound fresh large strawberries

8 ounces cream cheese (softened)

½ cup powdered sugar

1 teaspoon vanilla

Graham cracker crumbs (finely crushed)

Clean and prepare strawberries, leaving the leaves attached. Hollow out the center or cut berries into quarter wedges (do not cut all the way through). Stand strawberries in mini-muffin papers cut side up. Prepare filling: Cream together softened cream cheese, powdered sugar and vanilla until blended and smooth. Fill a pastry bag with the cream cheese mixture. Press cream cheese mixture into the cut out area in the strawberries until it is slightly above the tops of the fruit. Crush graham crackers into fine crumbs (or get ready prepared store-bought crumbs). Sprinkle crumbs over the tops of the berries and cream.

This is a pretty and elegant treat at any tea party. They are simple to make and delicious! For other ideas or variations on this, try using fresh peach wedges (to keep peaches from turning brown, sprinkle lemon juice over them or soak them in lemon water until ready to serve). Kiwis or pineapple would also be great using this recipe!

"Tea...wealth of the Earth. Blessed with the sweet spirit of Heaven."
DU YU—"ODE TO TEA"

-Week 18-

And thou shalt love the Lord thy God with all thine heart, and with all thy soul, and with all thy might. And these words, which I command thee this day, shall be in thine heart: and thou shalt teach them diligently unto thy children, and shalt talk of them when thou sittest in thine house, and when thou walkest by the way, and when thou liest down, and when thou risest up.

DEUTERONOMY 6:5-7

JIMMY AND JEREMY WERE STARTING TO GET OUT of control. They were eight years old and already starting to show signs of aggression and bullying. They were twins and very competitive and they often would dare each other to go up to some of the neighborhood kids and steal from them and knock them down. Then they would laugh when they made the other children cry.

The parents of other children would often come to the twin's mother and father and report their behavior and demand an apology and urge them to start disciplining their children before it was too late.

The twin's parents decided it was time to sit down with the boys and talk about what they thought the problem was. In thinking back over the past five years, they realized that since they had moved from another state, they failed to find a new church home. They weren't all that faithful before, but now their church attendance was non-existent. Not only were they not home for the boys because they both worked, but they failed to give them a moral upbringing by not attending church and making sure they taught them the right way to live and the consequences for their bad behavior.

So as the four of them sat down together, they got out their family Bible and dusted it off. They read over the Ten Commandments from the Old Testament and then the story of Jesus and how he died for their sins in the New Testament. They prayed together and made the decision that they would search diligently for a new church home and their boys would be taught right from wrong.

The boy's behavior didn't change overnight, but together, they began to think about why they did the things they did. Eventually the Lord touched their hearts and healed their souls. They stopped being bullies and ended their destructive ways and grew up to be godly men. One became a youth minister and the other a doctor, with families of their own. They continued what their parent's started so many years before. They had a daily devotional time with their own families and were faithful members of their churches and their children grew up knowing the Lord.

Father, help me to find time each day to sit down with my children, no matter how old they are and let them know how much I love them. Guide me in teaching them your ways, not only by my life, but also by your word. In Jesus name, I pray. Amen.

NOTES: _____

_____

_____

Cucumber Tea Sandwich

Peeled seedless cucumbers
½ cup of softened cream cheese
½ cup of chopped watercress leaves
Salt to taste
½ cup of chopped alfalfa sprouts (optional)
16 slices of white bread (or wheat or whole grain)

Hint: Freezing bread before preparing makes it easier to spread and cut.

Thinly slice the cucumber and place on paper towels to remove excess moisture. In a small bowl combine softened cream cheese and watercress. Spread on one side of each slice of bread. Lay cucumber slices on the cream cheese coated side of 8 slices of bread. Lightly salt to taste. Cover cucumbers with 1 tablespoon of the alfalfa sprouts (optional). Lay the remaining slices of bread on top of the sprouts and cucumbers, cream cheese side down.

Trim the crusts from the bread and cut the sandwiches diagonally in half, and then cut in half again to form triangular shaped tea sandwiches or cut them in quarters. Recipe yields 8 whole sandwiches, 16 halves, or 32 fourths.

This recipe can also be made using butter instead of the cream cheese.

Use only best quality bread for your sandwiches. This can also be made with whole grain or rye bread.

-Week 19-

Every word of God is pure: he is a shield unto them that put their trust in him. Add thou not unto his words, lest he reprove thee, and thou be found a liar. Two things have I required of thee; deny me them not before I die: Remove far from me vanity and lies: give me neither poverty nor riches; feed me with food convenient for me: lest I be full, and deny thee, and say, 'Who is the LORD'? Or lest I be poor, and steal and take the name of my God in vain.

PROVERBS 30:5-9

THE BOOK OF PROVERBS IS A WONDERFUL BOOK. It's full of choice bits of wisdom about how to live and how not to live. There is something for everyone and how to deal with every problem in life. The purpose of the book is to show that God is in control of life and knows what is best for us.

Solomon wrote the majority of the Proverbs, with the possible exceptions of chapters 30 and 31. Agur the son of Jakeh is credited for writing chapter 30. Not too much is known about Agur. Some have even speculated that Agur was another name for Solomon, possibly writing under an alias. At any rate, the verses 7-9 in this chapter, contains the only prayer in the whole book of Proverbs.

In going over these verses, if we were to break them down, he is saying that the word of God is true and pure and we can trust in them to be a shield against the devil. There is nothing we can add to what has been written to make them more true or discredit them. If we were to add to them, the things we say may not be in accordance with God's Word. If we were to take anything away from the Word, than we would be denying their truth.

Two things that Agur prays for in verse 8 are to remove him from vanity (pride of life) and lies and to make him neither too rich nor too poor. He only wants enough to satisfy him and meet his needs. He contends that if he is rich, he may not feel like he needs God, but on the other hand if he is too poor he may get into trouble, because he would have to steal and harm others by trying to get ahead. As a beggar he would be afraid that he would curse God and deny his existence.

What do you pray for? Do you ever pray that God will bless you with great riches or success? Or do you pray that God will meet your needs for that day. Like the manna that God sent to the children of Israel, they could only eat what they were given for one day and couldn't hold anything over to the next day because it would spoil. Besides, if you were to become rich and successful you would feel you no longer needed God to fill your needs on a daily basis.

Dear Heavenly Father, thank you for your true and living Word. Like Agur (Solomon?), help me to pray for just what I need to live each day. Help me not to be prideful if you were to give me success in my work, but to give you the credit for everything I do. As you prayed, 'Give us this day, our daily bread' let that be my prayer. You know what I have need of, and I trust that it will be done. In Jesus name, I pray. Amen.

NOTES: _____

_____

_____

Chicken Salad Tea Sandwich

2 cooked chicken breasts (Rotisserie Chicken is good)

½ cup halved seedless red grapes

¼ cups of chopped nuts

½ cup finely chopped celery

¼ cup finely chopped red onions (optional)

Salt and pepper to taste

Mayonnaise or salad dressing

16 slices of white or wheat bread (rye or whole grain would be good too)

Softened room-temperature butter

Freeze the bread for easier spreading and cutting. In a food processer on pulse or chop setting or by hand, finely chop the chicken. In a large bowl combine the chicken, grapes, nuts, celery, and onions. Add mayonnaise a little at a time until just moist and to your taste. Season with salt and pepper. Spread a thin layer of butter on each slice of bread. This will keep the moisture from the salad from soaking into the bread. Top the buttered side of 8 slices of bread with the chicken salad mixture. Then place the rest of the bread, butter side down on top of the salad. Trim the crust off the bread and cut in quarters. Recipe makes 8 whole sandwiches, 16 halves or 32 fourths. Place in airtight container and refrigerate until ready to serve.

This is a delicious spread for anytime. For a light lunch or supper idea, it is great on toasted bread served with a bowl of your favorite soup! It is also good as an appetizer served on crackers.

-Week 20-

*And he said, whereunto shall we liken the kingdom of
God? Or with what comparison shall we compare it? It
is like a grain of mustard seed, which, when it is sown
in the earth, is less than all the seeds that be in the earth:
But when it is sown, it growth up, and becometh greater
than all herbs, and shooteth out great branches; so that
the fowls of the air may lodge under the shadow of it.*

MARK 4:30-32

HAVE YOU EVER SEEN A MUSTARD SEED? If you have, you know that it is tiny! It is no bigger than the head of a pin and yet certain varieties of it (black mustard) can grow upwards to 9 feet tall, making it one of the largest herbs in the world.

In the Bible, Jesus compares the tiny seed to the growth of his kingdom. It started out small, but soon it would grow into a worldwide movement. When he speaks of the fowls of the air resting under it, he could have been referring to the Gentiles seeking refuge in the kingdom of God.

Jesus also said to his followers: *"If ye have faith as a grain of mustard seed, ye shall say unto this mountain, remove hence to yonder place; and it shall be removed; and nothing shall be impossible unto you." Matthew 17:20.* Again he uses the mustard seed as an illustration. He uses it to let people know that even the tiniest particle of faith, can be planted in someone and something beautiful and powerful can come from it. For the seed to grow, however, it needs to be planted in good soil (the Word of God), watered daily (through praise and prayer) and bask in the sunlight (fellowship with God and other Christians).

As the tiny seed of faith in God grows in you, others will be drawn to you because of your positive outlook on life. You may be just the one to move the mountain of disbelief in another person. We may not be able to do this by ourselves, but by trusting in God and allowing him to work through us, the seeds will be planted and God will do the harvesting. We just have to have the faith of a mustard seed.

Having afternoon teas and get-togethers with other Christians or with people interested in learning about more about Jesus, is a good way to plant the seeds of faith, and nourish each other's growth. It would also be a wonderful time to share key learning's from your Bible studies or share ways that you can start an outreach program.

Lord, give me the opportunity, courage, and will to reach out to others who are lacking faith. Help me to be the sower that spreads the seeds of faith to those around me. At the same time, help me to seek you more diligently, so that my own seed of faith continues to grow and blossom into something beautiful for you. In Jesus name, I pray. Amen.

NOTES: _____

_____

_____

"There is no trouble so great or grave that cannot be much diminished by a nice cup of tea."
BERNARD-PAUL HEROUX

Egg Salad Tea Sandwiches

8 hard-boiled eggs

½ cup mayonnaise

1 teaspoon mustard

1 tablespoon finely chopped dill or dill pickles (optional)

Room temperature butter

20 slices white or wheat bread

Peel eggs and coarsely chop. Put in medium size bowl. Mash into smaller bits with the back of a fork. Add mayonnaise, mustard and dill. Stir until fully mixed and even throughout. Spread each side of bread with a thin coat of butter. Place 2 tablespoons of egg salad on 10 slices of bread lay the rest of the bread on top of the slices. Trim off the crusts with a sharp knife and quarter the bread. Makes 40 quarter sandwiches, 20 halves or 10 whole. Store in airtight container in the refrigerator until ready to serve.

Hint: Freezing bread before serving makes it easier to spread and cut neatly.

Trivia: Mustard is made from grinding the mustard seeds into a fine powder and mixed with water, salt, and lemon juice or other liquids. The word mustard comes from the Latin: "mustum ardens" meaning "burning must". "Must" is a word that refers to the liquid it's mixed in.

-Week 21-

He answered and said unto them,' Give ye them to eat'. And they say unto him, 'Shall we go and buy two hundred pennyworth of bread, and give them to eat? He saith unto them, 'How many loaves have ye? Go and see'. And when they knew, they say 'Five, and two fishes'. And he commanded them to make all sit down by companies upon the green grass. And they sat down in ranks, by hundreds, and by fifties, And when he had taken the five loaves and the two fishes, he looked up to heaven, and blessed, and brake the loaves, and gave them to his disciples to set before them; and the two fishes divided he among them all. And they did all eat, and were filled.

MARK 6:37-42

THE ROAD WAS LONG AND DUSTY. MY FAMILY and I walked for hours and slept by the roadside at night to rest. Tomorrow we would complete our journey. We heard that there was a new prophet, a great teacher, that would be preaching and we wanted to see him. We didn't know where to go or how to find him, but as we drew closer to this large lake, we saw crowds of people coming toward us. We stopped one of men and asked him where the multitudes of people were going. He answered and said that they were following a man named Jesus and pointed to a boat out on the water. 'That's him and his men out there,' he said.

Excitedly, we turned and our strength had been restored, because today we knew we were going to finally see this man called Jesus. We continued to follow the crowd keeping one eye on the road ahead of us, and one eye on the boat. We wanted to make sure we were going to the right place. Our journey ended when we came to a small hill. The men had docked the boat that we saw on the lake. We were all crowding around it. The men told us all to back up and go rest on the side of the hill. Jesus would be going there and he would speak to us in that place.

We all ran to the hill and tried to find a good place to see him, but with everyone standing, it was hard to see him. It was wonderful listening to the Man of God speak, but it was getting close to lunchtime and everyone started complaining because they were getting hungry. We heard Jesus tell his men to go find food. We heard the disciples ask where they would find food enough to feed so large a crowd as this. He told them to go out to the people to see if anyone brought anything. Then he had everyone sit down in groups and had the disciples go around asking for food. I suddenly remembered that my son had brought 5 loaves of bread and 2 fishes with him for our dinner. He raised his hand, and was excited when the disciples came to him. He gladly gave them the food. Jesus instructed the disciples to get 12 baskets from the boat. When he blessed the food, a miracle happened. We saw him put loaves and fishes in each of the baskets and had the disciples go to every person on the hill to give them food and everyone had enough to eat. After our delicious dinner, they came around to gather the leftovers and they were astounded. They were able to gather enough to refill the baskets! After he was through preaching, he sent his disciples back to the boat to depart, and he had the crowd of people leave. Then he went off to a quiet place alone to pray. It had been a long day and many were saved that day, including my family. We knew that we had been in the presence of the Son of God, and his name was Jesus.

Dear Heavenly Father, thank you for your provisions and for your love towards us in knowing what we need. Thank you for a time of filling, not only with food, but also with your Word and Holy Spirit. In Jesus name, I pray. Amen.

Smoked Salmon Tea Sandwich

1 tablespoon finely chopped dill

1 teaspoon horseradish mustard

1 tablespoon finely chopped green onions or chives

¼ cup mayonnaise or salad dressing

16 slices of your choice of bread (whole grain, rye or pumpernickel works best or use 8 sliced mini bagels)

Softened butter

¼ pound thinly sliced smoked salmon

Endive leaves

Mix together the seasonings and mayonnaise together in a small bowl. Spread each slice of bread or mini-bagel with a thin layer of butter. Add a thin layer of the mayonnaise mixture to top of 8 slices of buttered bread. Top with thin slices of salmon and then with an endive leaf (you can use any kind of lettuce here if you wish). If using regular sandwich bread, cut off crust and cut bread in quarters. If you use bread that has been covered in grains, leave crust on for added crunch and flavor.

What a fun recipe to go with today's devotional. When you eat your Salmon Tea Sandwiches, remember the miracle of the loaves and fishes and the teachings of Jesus on the hillside!

"Remember the tea kettle, although it is up to its neck in hot water it keeps on singing."
AUTHOR UNKNOWN

-Week 22-

Now faith is the substance of things hoped for, the evidence of things not seen. For by it the elders obtained a good report. Through faith we understand that the worlds were framed by the word of God, so that things which are seen were not made of things which do appear.

HEBREWS 11:1-3

THE DEFINITIONS OF FAITH ARE: "CONFIDENCE OR TRUST in a person or thing, belief that is not based on proof, belief in God or in the doctrines or teaching of religion" (from dictionary.com)

Some people have referred to Hebrews 11 as the 'Faith Hall of Fame' chapter in the Bible. The people mentioned in the chapter were champions of exhibiting the faith Paul refers to in verse 1 and 2.

To start with, Abel offered a more perfect sacrifice to God through faith, giving the best he had to God, knowing that it was the right thing to do. Enoch pleased God, even though he did not see him, and his testimony was rewarded by not seeing death. By faith, Noah believed God when he told him that he was going to send the flood to destroy the world. Even though Noah had never seen rain, he believed him and followed his orders to build the ark and save his family and the animals. Abraham was called out to go to a land that he'd never been in before, taking Isaac and Jacob with him. Abraham's wife Sara also had faith and believed God when he told her she was going to have a child, even past her childbearing years. Abraham had faith when God tested him to offer up Isaac as a sacrifice. Isaac blessed Jacob and Esau concerning the things to come in their lives. When Jacob was dying he blessed the sons of Joseph. Joseph before he died mentioned that the children of Israel would be leaving Egypt. By faith, Moses, when he was grown, refused to be called the son of the Pharaoh's daughter, choosing to be afflicted with the people of God. Through faith, Moses kept the Passover, sprinkling blood on the lintel to protect the firstborn. By faith he led the children of God through the Red Sea on dry land. By faith the walls of Jericho fell down as they marched around it, blowing horns. Rahab by her faith was saved because she helped them. These are but a handful of people who had faith that God would lead them and protect them. The Bible is full of stories of people who believed through faith, without seeing. Christ himself said to Thomas: *'Because thou hast seen me, thou hast believed; blessed are they that have not seen, and yet have believed'.*

What about you? Do you believe and have faith in what you cannot see? I have to confess that sometimes I have problems with this, but even though I know Christ died for my sins and I have a head knowledge that he was an actual human being (albeit the Son of God), and I believe he lived over 2000 years ago, the reason I continue to believe in him and make him my Lord, is because he is alive in my heart.

Lord, although I believe in you, there are days when I feel so distant from you. Help me Lord to seek you in everything I do and trust that you will work everything out. Lord, grow my faith, just like that mustard seed, and make me stronger. Help me not only to trust you when I see visible results, but also when the answers are long in coming. In Jesus name, I pray. Amen.

NOTES: _____

_____

_____

Pimiento Cheese Sandwich

Spread

16 ounces of sharp cheddar cheese shredded	
1 (4 ounce) jar of undrained diced pimientos	
1 cup mayonnaise	
¾ cup of walnuts or pecans (toasted and chopped)	
Salt to taste	
¼ teaspoon hot sauce (optional)	

Cover and chill. Can be served with crackers, celery or sliced fruit or spread on bread.

Tea Sandwiches

16 slices of bread (white, wheat or whole grain)	
Softened butter	

Spread each slice of bread with a thin coat of butter. Spread 8 slices with the cheese mixture and lay the other slices over the tops. Trim the crust and quarter the bread. Makes 8 whole, 16 halves, or 32 quarter sandwiches.

Refrigerate sandwiches in airtight container until ready to serve. Refrigerate any leftover cheese spread.

Pimiento cheese spread is typically a Southern United States food. Variations in the spread can include adding chopped green onions or chives to the mixture. It can be made spicy by adding hot sauce and/or cayenne pepper.

-*Week 23*-

For God so loved the world, that he gave his only begotten Son, that whosoever believeth in him should not perish, but have everlasting life. For God sent not his Son into the world to condemn the world; but that the world through him might be saved.

JOHN 3:16-17

HE CAME TO JESUS IN THE NIGHT. HE was a Pharisee, a leader among the Jews, but he was afraid of what the others would say if they knew he was seeking out Jesus. He had to know, had to learn for himself why this man claimed to be the Son of God. He was curious. He had heard him speak and had seen the miracles that he had done and couldn't deny that God must have been with him. Jesus told him: "*Verily, verily, I say unto thee, except a man be born again, he cannot see the kingdom of God.*"

Surely a man cannot be born again when he is old and he can't go into his mother's womb again. He questioned Jesus. 'How can this be?'

Jesus replied, "*Except a man be born of water and of the Spirit, he cannot enter the Kingdom of God.*"

It was a hard concept for the Pharisee to understand. What was this man, Jesus, talking about? After a little while, he understood that being born of water referred to the physical act of childbirth, but being born of the Spirit, was harder for him to understand. In all of his years as being a Pharisee, this had never been taught to him. They taught the laws of

Moses. This thing about the Spirit was something new, something that was foreign to their teachings.

Jesus tried to explain what he was telling him, because he knew that he still didn't get it. *"The wind bloweth where it listeth, and thou hearest the sound thereof, but canst not tell whence it cometh, and wither it goeth: so is every one that is born of the Spirit."*

The wise teacher of the Jews still didn't quite understand. Jesus responded and told him that they heard what he had to say and witnessed the miracles that were done and they still didn't understand. How would they ever understand heavenly things? He told him that he came down from heaven, but soon he would be lifted up as Moses lifted up the serpent on a stick in the wilderness, signifying the kind of death he would be enduring to save those who believed on him.

Did Nicodemus understand and believe Jesus after their talk? In John, chapter 7, he tried to defend Jesus. Later in chapter 19, he brought spices and helped Joseph of Arimathaea prepare Jesus's body for burial. So again, did he believe? I would like to think so.

Dear Lord, thank you for your scriptures that give us hope for everything that we are facing today. Your Word is true and comforting. Thank you for your Holy Spirit that often speaks to our hearts when we question why things happen the way they do. Thank you for dying on the cross for our sins, so we can know eternal life. In Jesus name, I pray. Amen

NOTES: _____

_____

_____

Pineapple Tea Sandwiches

1 (8 ounce) can crushed pineapple	
2 tablespoons flour	
¾ cup finely chopped walnuts or pecans	
¾ cup of sugar	
1 ½ tablespoons mayonnaise or salad dressing	
1 loaf bread	

Mix all the ingredients except mayonnaise in a medium saucepan. Cook over low heat until thick and bubbly, stirring constantly. Remove from heat and allow to cool. After cooling, mix in mayonnaise or salad dressing. Cover and cool in refrigerator until ready to use. Freeze bread for easier cutting. Spread pineapple mixture on half of the slices of bread. Place another slice of bread on top. Trim crust and cut bread in quarters.

You can also use pineapple preserves in place of the pineapple/flour/sugar mixture. Just add nuts and mayonnaise to the preserves. To garnish it, place a pineapple cube on top of each quarter sandwich and attach it with a toothpick.

"So of all the particulars of health and exercise, and fit nutriment, and tonics. Some people will tell you there is a great deal of poetry and fine sentiment in a chest of tea."

RALPH WALDO EMERSON, LETTERS AND SOCIAL AIMS

-Week 24-

Let brotherly love continue. Be not forgetful to entertain
strangers: for thereby some have entertained angels
unawares.

HEBREWS 13: 1-2

Do you believe in angels? Do you believe they still exist? They are messengers of God and they appeared in the Bible 273 times! From their first presence in the book of Genesis in the Garden of Eden all the way through Revelation when John talks about their role at the end times, we see them. They not only brought messages from God, but they also ministered to people and in times of battle they helped fight on the side of believers. It was angels that guarded the gates of Eden. Angels in the form of men spoke with Abraham and later went to Sodom and Gomorrah to warn Lot about the coming destruction. They talked with the prophets. Gabriel told Mary that she was going to have a baby. On the night of his birth, there was a multitude of them telling the shepherds about the savior. When Jesus was in the wilderness, the angels ministered to him. In The Revelation of John, the angels would be heralding the end times by blowing trumpets, and they would also release the seven vials, and loose the seven seals.

When people depict angels in their art, they are shown to be larger than humans, radiant, and have two wings. When the Jewish people were to build the Ark of the Covenant, they were to depict angels (cherubim) with their wings pointing up to Heaven. Isaiah, when he saw the seraphim, they had 3 sets of wings.

People, when they have near death experiences, often tell of seeing angels helping them in the transition or the passing over into heaven.

Angels don't always appear as a heavenly vision, however. Sometimes they appear in human form, pretty much like you and me. God can send them in whatever form he wishes when he gives them a task to perform in our lives.

Do I believe in angels? I do. If I didn't believe in them they wouldn't have a role in my novels I write. I may have even had my own real life experience with them. Over thirty years ago, I had been praying for another child. I was having difficulty getting pregnant and it had been almost four years since my first daughter was born. One night, a young family came to my doorstep, barefoot and dirty. They said that they were parked next door but they had run low on gas and couldn't get to a store. They hadn't had anything to eat and were hungry. Somehow, we got around to talking about religion and about children. It was really strange. They said they knew about the Bible and then they reassured me that I would soon have a child. After they left, I quickly put some food in a bag for them and was going to take it over to where they said they parked. When I got there, they were gone. I had a strange feeling in my heart. Was I duped by strangers or were they messengers from God? The verse about entertaining angels unaware came into my mind. The following Sunday we had a church picnic on the grounds. The message that the preacher gave us that day was...you guessed it, about strangers and entertaining angels unaware. Two weeks following my visit by the strangers and the sermon by my pastor, I found out I was pregnant. So thirty plus years later, I still believe that angels visited me that night. My daughter, who is now thirty years old, is also an author like me. The protagonists in most of her books? Angels.

Dear Heavenly Father, thank you Lord for your angels,
and thank you that they still visit us and protect us. In
Jesus name, I pray. Amen

Club Sandwich

| 16 slices bacon (optional) |
| 24 slices of bread (white or wheat, traditional club sandwiches are made on toasted bread) |
| Mayonnaise |
| 16 lettuce leaves |
| 16 slices fully cooked deli meat (turkey is usually used, but you can substitute ham, roast, salami or other meat or a combination of meats) |
| 8 slices of Cheddar or Swiss cheese (optional) |
| Tomatoes and/or cucumbers sliced thin (optional) |

Cook bacon in heavy skillet. Toast bread (if desired). Spread a thin layer of mayonnaise or salad dressing on each slice of bread (you will use 3 slices of bread for each sandwich). Begin your layers: on first slice of bread place the turkey (or other deli meat), cheese, lettuce and cucumbers (optional). Top first layer with a slice of bread, mayonnaise side up. Next layer is for bacon and tomatoes, and then place third slice of bread over all with mayonnaise side down. Trim the crusts and quarter the sandwiches. Makes 8 whole, 16 halves, or 32 quarters. Secure each sandwich with an hors d'œrve stick (or fancy toothpick).

There are several versions of this popular sandwich and you can use these or any other ingredients as desired. Shown are the classic ingredients. You can use mustard as a condiment on these as well. They are usually made with toasted bread, and they have 2 layers separated by another slice of bread. These sandwiches had their beginnings in the late 19th century.

-Week 25-

Whereby are given unto us exceeding great and precious promises: that by these ye might be partakers of the divine nature, having escaped the corruption that is in the world through lust. And beside this, giving all diligence, add to your faith virtue; and to virtue knowledge; and to knowledge temperance; and to temperance patience; and to patience godliness; and to godliness brotherly kindness; and to brotherly kindness charity. For if these things be in you, and abound, they make you that ye shall neither be barren nor unfruitful in the knowledge of our Lord Jesus Christ.

2 PETER 1:4-8

'PROMISES, PROMISES,' WE SIGH, WHEN STILL ANOTHER PROMISE given to us is broken. We begin to wonder if anyone can be trusted anymore. Our politicians are notorious for promising us a better life if we put our faith in them and vote them into office. Then as soon as they are elected they turn their back on almost everything they said and become self-serving or side with anything that is 'popular' at the moment and will lead to them getting more power. But they aren't the only ones. What about our coworkers and our boss? The company promises that we will have job security and promotions and pay increases. Then that doesn't pan out. The company may be taken over by someone else and we lose our seniority and not only do we not get that raise, but we could actually be cut due to downsizing. We have no control over our politicians (except by voting them out at the next election) or over our job situation, except either by accepting the new situation, or finding another job and starting over.

But what if the promises made were from our parents, children, or spouse? What then? Those unkept promises hurt the worst. Our parents make promises to us that we will always be looked after and that they will always be there for us. They can't always keep those promises. There may be circumstances where they find they can't always be there for us, no matter how much they want to be. They expect us to grow and not need them so much. How many times have your children made promises they couldn't keep. They promise to stick to their curfew, they promise to get better grades, they promise to clean their room, and they promise to never hang out with the wrong crowd or get involved in drugs or alcohol, and our spouses, at our wedding, how they promised to love and cherish us the rest of our lives until death us do part. You get the idea. Promises, everyone makes them including us. How many promises have you made that fell through the proverbial 'cracks' and you were unable to fulfill them?

But what of God's promises? He is faithful. He is probably the only one that ever followed through on all his promises and we can have confidence that he will continue to keep those promises in our lives. Are you trusting in him today to act on his promises in your life?

Dear Lord, thank you for your promises that you gave us in your word. We know that you are able to keep those promises to us. Forgive us Lord where we failed to live up to our end of the bargain and made promises that we were unable to keep both towards you and to others in our life. Help us always to follow your example and be trustworthy in all things. In Jesus name, I pray. Amen

NOTES: _____

_____

_____

God's Promises Cookies

3 egg whites

¾ cup sugar

½ cup melted butter

¼ teaspoon vanilla

¼ teaspoon almond extract

1 cup flour

2 tablespoons water.

Prepare several Bible verse references, 1 on each slip of paper. Paper should be ¼ inch by 1 ¾ to fit inside cookie.

Preheat oven to 375 degrees F. Prepare cookie sheet with cooking spray or line with parchment paper (this works best). In a large bowl whip egg whites and sugar on high speed with mixer until frothy. Add next 5 ingredients one at a time and mix well after each. Batter should be the consistency of pancake batter. Spoon batter on prepared cookie sheets in a 3-inch circle. Leave enough room between each for spreading while baking (approximately two inch spaces). Bake 5-7 minutes or until edges are slightly brown. Remove cookies 1 at a time and place strip of paper with verse in the middle of the cookie. Fold cookie in half over the paper and then fold the ends together to form the "fortune cookie shape". Quickly do this with the rest of the cookies while they are still warm and pliable. If they don't close properly you can place them in a muffin tin for them to hold their shape until cool.

This would be a fun recipe to use for Vacation Bible School or any Bible themed party. Great for afternoon teas with Jesus!

-Week 26-

Hast thou not known? Hast thou not heard, that the everlasting God, the LORD, the Creator of the ends of the earth, fainteth not, neither is weary? There is no searching of his understanding. He giveth power to the faint; and to them that have no might he increaseth strength. Even the youths shall faint and be weary, and the young men shall utterly fall: But they that wait upon the LORD shall renew their strength; they shall mount up with wings as eagles; they shall run, and not be weary; and they shall walk, and not faint.

ISAIAH 40:28-31

IT HAD BEEN A LONG DAY AND MAGGIE was tired. She was a nurse in the intensive care unit at the hospital where she worked. It was particularly trying because one her patients that she had been caring for, had died. She knew she did everything she could to care for her, but even in the best of times it was something that she couldn't control. The woman was just too ill. She beat herself up wondering if she could have done anything different to achieve a different outcome. No one blamed her, but she still felt uneasy and sad about the situation. The rest of the day didn't get any better. She couldn't wait until she got home and shake off the helpless feeling. After she was home, she was about to take a long hot bath to unwind when the doorbell rang.

Her next-door neighbor brought her a gift basket with a box of herbal tea, some fresh baked scones, still warm from the oven, and a jar of fresh homemade strawberry jam. Tucked inside the basket was a small devotional book. On the cover of the book there was a picture of an eagle with the verse found in Isaiah 40: 31.

Through her tears, Maggie invited her neighbor in and put on the teakettle. While they were waiting on the familiar whistle announcing that the water was hot, they sat down and talked.

Her neighbor told her that the woman who died that day was her aunt and she heard from her mother about how hard it was on Maggie when she passed away.

Her neighbor went on to tell her how sick her aunt had been and how she often prayed for Jesus to take her home. "It was a blessing for her to go in the presence of someone who really cared for her," she said. Then she went on to thank her for taking such good care of her beloved aunt.

After the water came to a boil, Maggie poured the water over the tea bags in her teapot and set the table with her finest china and put the basket of scones and jelly in the center of the table. As she visited with her neighbor, the sadness melted away as she shared stories about her aunt's life. The neighbor said that whenever her aunt felt down she would sit awhile with a cup of tea, a treat, and a good devotional book and prayed until she felt better. Maggie had to agree that it was a wonderful idea, because as it turned out, this would be the first afternoon of many years to come to visit with her new friend and neighbor over a cup of tea.

Lord, sometimes things don't always turn out the way we want them to. Unhappy or stressful events can make us weary. Often we become tired or depressed and feel hopeless. Lord when that happens that's when we need to turn to you all the more. Help us always to remember we can find comfort in you. In Jesus name, I pray. Amen.

NOTES: _____

_____

_____

Mini Quiches

2 sheets of ready-made puff pastry or small pastry tart shells

Finely chopped green onions or chopped fresh chives

4 slices of diced bacon (optional)

2 whole large eggs beaten

½ cup cream

½ cup milk

½ cup shredded cheddar cheese

2 tablespoons chopped fresh parsley

Salt and pepper to taste.

If using puff pastry, cut circles about 3 inches in diameter. Line a greased mini-muffin tin and line the tin with the pastry circles. Sauté the onions (or chives) and bacon bits until cooked through (about 3 minutes). Mix all of the ingredients together and season to taste. Spoon the mixture into the shells and bake in a 350-degree F. oven for 20 minutes or until set.

Many people think that the Quiche is a French dish, but did you know that it was originally German? It comes from the German word Kuchen (sounds like Kitchen, um...). The type in this recipe is Quiche Lorraine because it contains bacon and cheese. Its origins are from the Lorraine region of France. Other varieties of Quiches are quiche au champignons (with mushrooms) or Florentine (with spinach) or Provençale (with tomatoes).

-Week 27-

Ho, every one that thirsteth, come ye to the waters, and
he that hath no money; come ye, buy, and eat; yea,
come, buy wine and milk without money and without
price. Wherefore do ye spend money for that which is
not bread? And your labour for that which satisfieth
not? Hearken diligently unto me, and eat ye that which
is good, and let your soul delight itself in fatness.

ISAIAH 55: 1-2

WHEN JESUS WAS IN THE WILDERNESS AND WAS tempted by Satan to turn the stones into bread. He responded by saying '*Man shall not live by bread alone, but by every word that proceedeth out of the mouth of God*'.

It has been said that the best things in life are free. I would have to agree with that. You can't buy a smile, you can't buy love, and you can't buy the happy coincidences in your life. You can't buy the sight of our beautiful world or the stars and moon at night. You can't buy the sounds of laughter or the giggles of children at play. You can't buy the smell of fragrant flowers or perfume as their odors permeate the air. You can't buy the taste of your favorite foods...and you can't buy the love of God. God's blessings and his mercy are free! We don't even have to work for our salvation. It is the gift of God, paid for on the cross by Jesus. All we have to do is believe.

Are you thirsty? You can drink water or tea or any other beverage but these will only satisfy you for a short time. When Jesus talked with the Samaritan woman at the well in John 4:13, he told her, *'Whosoever drinketh of this water shall thirst again: but whosoever drinketh of the water that I shall give him shall never thirst; but the water that I shall give him shall be in him a well of water springing up into everlasting life'.*

Are you hungry? You can eat the bread or another food and a little while later you are hungry again. In John 6:35 Jesus said, *'I am the bread of life: he that cometh to me shall never hunger; and he that believeth on me shall never thirst'.*

Our bodies are amazing things. God gave us five senses to enjoy everything around us. Even in our afternoon teas, we see our friends and the pretty china and flowers; we listen to our friend's conversations and laugher; we smell the aroma of the tea, spices, and flowers; and we taste the foods that are placed before us. Even though some of these things were bought, the most important things in our afternoon tea are the fellowship we have with one another and with God, and those things are free.

Dear Heavenly Father, thank you for your Word. When I am thirsty, it quenches my thirst. When I am hungry, it fills me with joy. Lord, help me to realize that money can't buy me happiness and it can't be found in owning more things. The only way my happiness is complete is by trusting in you for all my needs. Thank you Lord for my five senses that I might enjoy all things. Thank you for paying the price for my sins that I can enjoy your forgiveness today and look forward to tomorrow. In Jesus name, I pray. Amen.

NOTES: _____

_____

_____

Crostini Spread Hors d'oeurve

8 ounces of cream cheese (softened)
1 cup sour cream
1 jar (6 ounces) marinated artichoke hearts, drained and chopped (or chopped olives or pickled banana peppers would also be good in this)
2 green onions or fresh chives divided)
Chopped cherry or plum tomatoes
1 loaf French bread, cut into 36 slices, toasted

Slice and toast French bread in oven at 400 degrees F until toasted on both sides. If you desire, you can brush on some olive oil on each slice before toasting.

To make spread: Beat cream cheese and sour cream in medium bowl with whisk until blended. Stir in chopped artichoke hearts (or olives or peppers) and ½ of the onions (or chives). Refrigerate until chilled. Spread cooled slices of bread with mixture and top with tomatoes and rest of onions or chives. Makes 36 hors d'oeurves.

'Crostini' is an Italian word for little toast.

Hors d'oeurve is a French phrase meaning set apart from the main work (meal). It is sometimes considered the first course of a meal or it can be serve as an appetizer. It is usually considered a finger food (eaten without utensils) and often served with cocktails or at tea parties or showers.

-Week 28-

Behold, what manner of love the Father hath bestowed upon us, that we should be called the sons of God: Therefore the world knoweth us not, because it knew him not. Beloved, now are we the sons of God, and it doth not yet appear what we shall be: but we know that, when he shall appear, we shall be like him; for we shall see him as he is.

1 JOHN 3:1-3

EVER SINCE THE TIME OF CHRIST, HIS FOLLOWERS have been persecuted. John the Baptist was beheaded, some of Christ's apostles were killed or imprisoned for their beliefs, his disciples were scattered and murdered. Some of them, like Stephen, became martyrs.

Later, a little further down the road of history, Nero, the Roman Emperor persecuted Christians. This was just the beginning. Time after time over the next two thousand years, hundreds of thousands Christians were killed because of their beliefs.

Today, even in our age of 'enlightenment', Christians around the world are persecuted or killed because they worship our Savior.

In America, with our freedom to worship Christ, we are very fortunate. We can meet together in churches without the fear of the government coming in to destroy us, at least for now. Other countries are not so fortunate. We always hear in the news about people being killed and whole churches being wiped out. Our missionaries are often at risk for their lives when they spread the gospel. Even though we have religious freedom, we often see organizations trying to erode away our Christian way of life. They've taken prayer and the Bible out of schools and other government organizations. Christmas and Easter have become just 'holidays' and not religious celebrations. We can no longer have manger scenes and crosses in public places. The Ten Commandments, the moral laws of all religions, can no longer be displayed in our government buildings.

So how can the world have so much hatred for Christians when all we want to do is worship Christ and the fact that through his death, we are forgiven of our sins and promised a home in Heaven? It is because the world is under control of Satan and he hates what Jesus had done to save us. Unless the world comes to the saving knowledge of Christ, the world will continue to persecute the church of believers.

What can we do about this? We can remember that we as Christians are set apart from the world. The world cannot steal our souls because we belong to Christ. We can spread the gospel of love to a world who needs to hear it before it's too late. We can be thankful for being saved and know that one day we will be taken out of this world and we will be like him when we enter into his glory.

Thank you Father for your assurance that you will be with us through the troubling times when it seems that the entire world hates us. Thank you Lord for saving me and all my fellow Christians. I pray for protection for those that are persecuted around the world. Help me to remember that the world is not my home, but my home is with you. In Jesus name, I pray. Amen.

NOTES: _____

_____

_____

Pea and Ricotta Bruschetta

Topping

1 ½ cups fresh or frozen peas (8 ounces)

1 tablespoon olive oil

1 ½ teaspoons coarsely chopped fresh mint leaves

2/3 cup ricotta cheese

¼ teaspoon salt

1/8 teaspoon pepper

Radishes (thinly sliced)

Bread

Italian bread cut into ½ inch slices

2 tablespoons olive oil

Salt and pepper

1 clove of garlic

Preheat oven to 400 degrees F. Slice bread and lay slices on a grill pan or cookie sheet. Lightly brush each slice with olive oil. Season the bread with salt and pepper. Toast the bread on each side, about 2-3 minutes per side. Rub the oiled and seasoned side with a clove of garlic after toasting. Set aside while you are making the topping.

Topping: Cook peas in a medium saucepan of salted water until they're bright green and just cooked through, about 2-4 minutes. Drain and place in a medium bowl. Season with more salt and pepper to taste. Add olive oil and chopped fresh mint leaves to peas and stir to combine. Crush mixture gently with the back of a fork. Set pea mixture aside. Place the ricotta cheese in a small bowl and season with the measured salt and pepper.

To serve: spread ricotta cheese on toast and spoon on the pea mixture evenly over the cheese. Top with the radishes.

-Week 29-

Let love be without dissimulation. Abhor that which is evil; cleave to that which is good. Be kindly affectioned one to another with brotherly love; in honor preferring one another; not slothful in business; fervent in spirit; serving the Lord; rejoicing in hope; patient in tribulation; continuing instant in prayer; distributing to the necessity of saints; given to hospitality.

ROMANS 12:9-13

PROVERBS 31:10-31, IN THE OLD TESTAMENT, DESCRIBES A virtuous woman. King Lemuel (another name for Solomon?) says that her husband trusts her. She is a diligent worker and businesswoman and makes clothes to sell in the market. She also makes clothes for her and her family. She plants a garden and feeds her family so they are never hungry. She reaches out to the needy and helps them. She is wise and kind. She is not lazy and makes sure her family has everything they need. Her husband and children rise up and call her blessed. She believes that favor and beauty is vain, and above all, she fears the Lord.

Romans 12:9-13 is very similar to the passage in Proverbs. It is referring to the virtuous Christian. Paul says that love should be truthful. There should be no deceit in perfect love. We should hate sin and stay far away from it. In all things we should find the good and cleave to it. We should love one another and as Jesus said in the 'golden rule': 'to do unto others as you would have them do unto you'. Paul takes it a step further saying that we should treat others better than we treat ourselves. We should be diligent in all good works and be excited about everything we do for the Lord. We are to be patient and kind and rejoice in the hope that is in us. We need to be always ready to pray. As much as is in us, we should help the less fortunate people in our lives through caring and prayer, and sometimes even in material needs. As good Christians, we should be hospitable and always welcoming others into our homes and lives.

When this passage was written soon after the crucifixion and resurrection, the apostles, including Paul, would go from town to town and teach the people everywhere they went about Christ. They were often tired and weary, but they knew some people who loved the Lord would offer them a room to stay and food to eat. We don't have quite the same culture in our present day but sometimes we have an opportunity to meet the needs of someone passing through town without money and a place to stay, someone like a visiting missionary or pastor, or possibly a college student that is in-between looking for apartments, or a young family that is moving into the area and is waiting on a place to rent. The best way to find opportunities to share your life and home with others is to check with your church. The pastor may have a list of folks that would love or need your hospitality.

Heavenly Father, help me to be willing and open to finding ways that I can help others in need. Let me always look for the good in people and treat them the way I would like to be treated. Give me the strength to be fervent in my spirit when it comes to being a servant for you. In Jesus name, I pray. Amen.

NOTES: _____

_____

_____

Tomato and Balsamic Bruschetta

1 loaf French bread

2 cloves of garlic

1 (8 ounce) cream cheese softened

16 cherry or plum tomatoes

½ cup sliced red onions

2 tablespoons balsamic vinegar

1 tablespoon olive oil

1 teaspoon brown sugar

1/8 teaspoon of salt

1/8 teaspoon of pepper

¼ cup of fresh chopped basil leaves

Preheat oven to 400 degrees F. Slice bread into 16 slices. Place on cookie sheet in a single layer. Toast each side until lightly browned (about 3-4 minutes per side). Rub each slice with garlic. Let cool.

Whisk together the vinegar, olive oil, brown sugar, salt and pepper (you can also use balsamic vinaigrette dressing in place of this).

Thinly slice the red onions and cut the cherry tomatoes in half or quarter the plum tomatoes.

To assemble, spread the toasted bread (garlic side up) with the cream cheese. Top with tomatoes and red onions and chopped basil. Drizzle vinegar and oil mixture over the top.

-Week 30-

*Verily, verily, I say unto you, he that believeth on me
hath everlasting life. I am that bread of life. Your fathers
did eat manna in the wilderness, and are dead. This
is the bread which cometh down from heaven, that a
man may eat thereof, and not die. I am the living bread,
which came down from heaven: if any man eat of this
bread, he shall live forever: and the bread that I will give
is my flesh, which I will give for the life of the world.*

JOHN 6:47-51

THE PEOPLE THAT WERE WITH JESUS ON THE day that he spoke with
them and were fed with the loaves and fishes were eager to see him
again. They stood on the shore as the disciples had boarded their boat
to go to the other side of the Sea of Galilee to Capernaum, but where was
Jesus? They wanted to see him again, but he wasn't with his men. Sadly
they turned and left to go home.

While out on the sea that night, a storm came up suddenly and the
waves were huge and rocked the boat relentlessly and the disciples were
afraid. Where was Jesus when they needed him? As they looked out on
the rough sea, they saw what they thought was an apparition coming
towards them. Were their eyes deceiving them? Did they long to see Jesus
so much that they were imagining him coming to them to protect them
from the sea that was about to destroy them? As he came closer to the
boat, they became afraid. Who was this person who could quite literally

walk on the water in the middle of a storm? As he came closer to the boat, Peter, always the outspoken one of the group, wanted to test the person claiming to be Jesus. He said: *'Lord if it be thou, bid me come unto thee on the water'*. Jesus told him to come. He got out of the boat and walked a few feet, but then became afraid as the winds picked up and he took his eyes off Jesus. He started to sink and cried out to him to save him. Jesus held out his hand to Peter to keep him from drowning and reproved him because of his lack of faith. After they came into the ship together, the wind ceased and the seas became still. Then the men in the ship worshipped him and said that truly he was the Son of God.

When they arrived on the other side of the sea, people came from miles around because they had heard about all of miracles that he had performed.

What is your relationship with Christ like? Do you search for Jesus because you believe that he can provide miracles in your life? Do you think he deserted you because you can no longer see or feel him in your heart? Are you like Peter and are gung-go about your beliefs, but when the first problem arises, you take your eyes off of him and worry that he can't help you? Where are you in your fellowship with him? Because the disciples saw the miracles, they believed. How much better is it for us to believe through faith that he is still performing miracles in our lives? We need to keep our eyes on him. He will save us in the end, even when we think there is no hope.

Lord, help me believe. Even though you are not physically in my presence, I know you are there spiritually and have performed miracles in my life because you made me your child and I know you love me. Thank you for always being there for me. In Jesus name, I pray. Amen.

NOTES: _____

_____

_____

Homemade Devonshire Cream

There are a few different ways you can make this homemade cream. The following recipes are just two of them. What they have in common is heavy cream (whipping cream or sour cream), cream cheese, and white sugar (regular or powdered). In England this is also sometimes called clotted cream (made from heated whole milk cream). It is extremely rich and is wonderful on biscuits or scones or as a dip for fruit.

Recipe #1:

1 (3 ounce) package of cream cheese

1 tablespoon sugar

1 cup heavy cream (whipping cream)

Dash of salt

Cream sugar, salt and cream cheese together until light and fluffy. Beat in cream until stiff peaks form. Keep in refrigerator until time to serve. Serves 16.

Recipe #2

1 -8 ounce package of cream cheese

½ cup sour cream

2 tablespoons of confectionary sugar

Cream sugar and cream cheese together until well blended. Add the sour cream and continue beating until smooth and creamy. Refrigerate until serving. This is wonderful on biscuits or scones with or without fruit or jam.

-Week 31-

I will bless the Lord, who hath given me counsel: my reins also instruct me in the night seasons. I have set the LORD always before me: because he is at my right hand, I shall not be moved. Therefore my heart is glad, and my glory rejoiceth: my flesh also shall rest in hope.

PSALMS 16:7-9

JENNIFER WAS HAVING PROBLEMS SLEEPING. SHE COULDN'T QUITE put her arms around the problem. She tried to see a doctor about it, but all he did was prescribe some medicine to help her relax. It helped for a little while, but she had to keep increasing her dose to make it work. The next day at work she would find herself 'hung over' from the medicine and could barely make it through the day. It was becoming a vicious cycle, trying to sleep at night and stay awake during the day. After a while she could barely function at all.

One day she decided that she just needed a break. She had thought about going to a psychiatrist to see if there was a reason she couldn't rest, but she didn't want to discuss her problems with a total stranger. She thought about talking with her family or her friends, but again, she didn't want them to think she was crazy. So she finally decided that she just needed to get away from it all for a time of rest and self-reflection. She didn't have the money to spend on a vacation so she chose a little corner of her home and made it into a retreat. She set a large comfortable chair by a window that faced out toward the woods behind her house.

She placed her favorite colorful cushions in the chair. On a small table next to the chair were her Bible and a beautiful bouquet of fragrant flowers from her garden. She enclosed the area to separate it from the rest of the house by placing a partition around her 'get-away'.

After setting up her 'retreat' she made a big pot of tea and opened the bag of gourmet cookies she had just bought for the occasion. She proceeded to pull out her best china. Nothing would be too good for her mini-vacation.

She had opened the window and with the breezes blowing gently through her hair, she was magically transported through time and space. She closed her eyes and imagined that she was sitting at the feet of Jesus as he preached on the side of the hill, delivering his sermon on the mount. Jesus was so close, she could almost reach out and touch him. As she thought of the words: *'Take therefore no thought for the morrow; for the morrow shall take thought for the things of itself. Sufficient unto the day is the evil thereof'*, she started to realize that the reason she had a hard time going to sleep was because she was always worrying about things. She had taken her eyes off Jesus and thought that she had to solve her own problems. Every night when she lay in her bed, she would fret over something that wasn't done that day or what was going to happen tomorrow. She worried about what would happen to her if she lost her job and how she would take care of herself. She confessed that she had taken her eyes off her Lord and his ability to meet her every need. After she realized what her problem was, she knelt down beside her chair and turned all of her life and worries over to God. She relinquished the fear and anxiety that kept her awake at night and put them in his hands. That night, for the first time in many months, Jennifer fell into a deep and restful sleep.

> *Dear Father in Heaven, help me realize that I have little, or no control over what may happen in my life. I need to always place my trust in you. You know what's going to happen and all my worrying isn't going to change anything. I turn it all over to you. In Jesus name, I pray. Amen.*

Canapés

Canapés is a type of hors d'oeuvre or appetizer. It is usually a decorative bite to eat. It is a finger food in that it normally is held in the hand and eaten in one bite. It is usually a spicy or salty food served on crackers or bread. The bread is often cut into shapes.

Base

Any type of cracker,

Or bread (deep fried, sautéed, or toasted).
Cut the bread in whatever shape you want. It can be made more decorative by using shaped cookie cutters.

Or you can use puff pastries or baked mini tart shells

Spread

Flavored cream cheese or butter. Flavor by adding your favorite spices, such as chives, dill, parsley, or sage, to the cream cheese or butter and blend it into a mixture.

The spread is more decorative if you pipe it on the toast or cracker with a pastry bag.

Toppings (garnishes)

You can decorate your canapés with chopped vegetables, herbs, fish, meat, cheese, caviar, or chopped nuts. Let your imagination go wild here!

See photo for ideas on how they can look with different toppings.

-Week 32-

Not that I speak in respect of want: for I have learned, in whatsoever state I am, therewith to be content. I know both how to be abased, and I know how to abound: everywhere and in all things I am instructed both to be full and to be hungry, both to abound and to suffer need. I can do all things through Christ, which strengtheneth me.

PHILIPPIANS 4:11-13

Paul, in writing to the church in Philippi, no doubt thought back to earlier times in his life, as well as what his life was like at the time of his writings.

He had grown up in Tarsus, the son of a Pharisee. Tarsus was a thriving seaport back in his day and was the center of a major university and a center of commerce. Paul probably grew up in a wealthy home and had the best education that he could get at that time. He even prided himself as being a 'Pharisee of Pharisees'. He even went so far as to assist in the murders of the new upstart followers of 'The Way', disciples who believed that this 'radical' prophet, Jesus, was the Son of God. Paul was a Jew living in the Roman Empire, so he bragged about being a Roman citizen as well as being a Jew.

Shortly after the death and resurrection of Christ, Paul was on his way to Damascus. He was going there to persecute more Christians. If anyone should have been condemned to die as an unbeliever and a murderer, it would have been Paul, but Jesus saw the great potential in him. He needed a man with the zeal that he had, to spread the gospel to other lands, not only to his fellow Jews, but also to the Gentiles. After Jesus confronted him on the road to Damascus, he saved him, but Paul had to be a willing follower of him. Paul's name was changed from Saul to Paul to signify the change in his life.

After Paul became an apostle and during his ministry he was beaten, rejected by many, laughed at, and thrown out on the streets. I'm sure that there were times when he was tired and hungry and longing for the love of others. Later in his life he was imprisoned on different occasions and almost died in a shipwreck. He was eventually martyred for his faith. So when he tells the Philippians that 'he can do all things through Christ who strengthens him', I believe him!

As a new Christian writer, sometimes I become discouraged. My number one goal is always to bring honor to God. I try to write books that bring inspiration to others so they will want to seek and learn more about God. Sometimes I get glowing reviews and I am encouraged to write more and even better stories, but sometimes people are not so nice in their reviews. They think they are being helpful, and often times they are, but it doesn't make the criticism go down any easier. I need to be more like Paul. I need to learn from my mistakes, shake the dust of rejection off my feet and be determined to continue to improve and above all to keep telling others about Christ in the best way I can.

How do you handle life's upsets? Do you claim the strength of Jesus to see you through the hard times and thank him for the good times?

Heavenly Father, thank you for all the good and bad things that happen in my life. The good things that happen encourage me, but the bad things can also be a source of learning and growing in strength of spirit and dependence on you. In Jesus name, I pray. Amen

NOTES: _____

_____

_____

Baked Cheese Straws

2/3 cup of all-purpose flour

3 tablespoons butter, diced

1 ½ ounces of sharp cheddar cheese finely grated

1 large egg

1 teaspoon of mustard

¼ teaspoon each of salt and pepper (you can use cayenne pepper for a little heat, if desired)

Preheat oven to 350 degrees F. Line cookie sheet with parchment paper or spray with cooking spray. Sift flour, salt, and pepper together into a bowl. Add butter, and mix until it resembles course breadcrumbs. Stir in the cheese. Lightly beat the egg and mustard together. Stir half of the egg mixture into the cheese and flour until it forms a smooth ball of dough. Roll dough into a 6-inch square. Cut into strips about ½ inch wide. Twist strips if desired. Place on baking sheet and brush on the remaining egg/mustard mixture. Bake for about 12 minutes or until golden brown.

Delicious with afternoon teas or anytime! Try serving these with salsa or marinara sauce for an extra flavor treat!

"I am so fond of tea that I could write a whole dissertation on its virtues. It comforts and enlivens without the risks attendant on spirituous liquors. Gentle herb! Let the florid grape yield to thee. Thy soft influence is a more safe inspirer of social joy"
JAMES BOSWELL, LONDON JOURNAL, 1762-1763

-Week 33-

Make a joyful noise unto the LORD, all ye lands. Serve the LORD with gladness: come before his presence with singing. Know ye that the LORD he is God: it is he that hath made us, and not we ourselves; we are his people, and the sheep of his pasture. Enter into his gates with thanksgiving, and into his courts with praise: be thankful unto him, and bless his name. For the LORD is good; his mercy is everlasting; and his truth endureth to all generations.

PSALM 100: 1-5

"GOD IS GOOD ALL THE TIME, ALL THE time God is good!" Our youth pastor proclaimed at the beginning of each of our worship services. He would have us repeat the refrain after him each time. It was to help us redirect our thoughts and focus on the service to come. By redirecting our thoughts, we would forget the trials and tribulations of the week since the last time we came together and forget the petty incidents and arguments we may have had with our families prior to arriving at the church.

It is not always easy to be joyful when we come to worship our Lord and Savior and if we are truthful, sometimes we are not always in a worshipful mood. Sometimes we are not feeling well, or have personal problems. Maybe we had a bad week at work and argued with our boss and are afraid that our job is in jeopardy. Maybe we just learned that someone we love has become ill and is in the hospital. We can't muster up a smile, let alone proclaim that 'God is good all the time'. We are just not feeling it. What then? What do we do when God seems so far away and when he seemingly doesn't care about what happens to us? Do we just throw away our fellowship with him? Do we inwardly proclaim that he is not good all the time? Do we stop worshipping because we are no longer thankful for his blessings?

This is hard. I've been there. I confess that I'm not perfect and yes, I don't always feel like rejoicing and praising God. Sometimes when we are at our lowest places in our lives, that's exactly the time that God is preparing to do great things through us.

The apostle Paul wrote in Romans 5:3-6: *'And not only so, but we glory in tribulations also: knowing that tribulation worketh patience; and patience, experience; and experience, hope: and hope maketh not ashamed; because the love of God is shed abroad in our hearts by the Holy Ghost which is given unto us'.*

So go ahead and proclaim that 'God is good all the time' because he is. Although it's hard to be thankful for our problems, if we realize that God is there for us and wants what is best for us, we can truly thank him for his love and goodness. Our problems are temporary. Our God is eternal and is eternally there for us!

> *Thank you Lord for your goodness and mercy. Even when we are unlovely and not thankful, you are still there. When we are your children, you want what's best for us. For that we can praise you and thank you even in the darkest times because we know you love us. In Jesus name I pray, Amen.*

NOTES: _____

_____

_____

Pecan Pralines

2 cups of light brown sugar packed
2 cups of sugar
1 cup of half and half
3 cups of coarsely chopped pecans
4 tablespoons of butter
1 teaspoon vanilla

Combine the sugars and the half and half in a heavy saucepan. Cook and stir occasionally over medium heat until it comes to a boil and reaches 227 degrees F. per candy thermometer or a soft ball stage (a soft ball stage can be tested by dropping a spoonful of the hot mixture into a bowl of cold water. If it is done, it will easily work into a ball with your fingers while in the water, and will flatten out when it is removed). Add pecans, vanilla and butter. Continue cooking and stirring frequently until butter is melted and blended in thoroughly. Remove pan from heat and let rest for 2 minutes. Using a tablespoon, scoop rounded spoons of mixture unto wax paper, leaving 2-3 inches between each ball of sugar mixture, as they will spread out. Let cool until firm.

For a more maple flavor, use maple extract in the place of the vanilla.

"The scattered tea goes with the leaves and every day a sunset dies."
WILLIAM FAULKNER

-Week 34-

And the angel answered and said unto the women, 'Fear not ye: for I know that ye seek Jesus, which was crucified. He is not here: for he is risen, as he said. Come, and see the place where the Lord lay. And go quickly, and tell his disciples that he is risen from the dead: and, behold, he goeth before you into Galilee; there shall ye see him: lo, I have told you'. And they departed quickly from the sepulcher with fear and great joy; and did run to bring his disciples word. And as they went to tell his disciples, behold, Jesus met them, saying, 'All hail'. And they came and held him by the feet, and worshipped him.

MATTHEW 28:5-9

A S I WRITE THIS, IT IS GOOD FRIDAY. My heart is focused on my Lord today. In my mind I go back in time to almost two thousand years ago. I visualized myself as one of the women following the ministry of our Savior; the man who we hoped would become our new king and free us from the tyranny of Rome. Now after being mobbed in the crowd and shoved aside and listening to rabid people screaming to crucify him, I crumbled to the ground in anguish. There was nothing his disciples and I could do to prevent this from happening. We were too outnumbered by those who would have him put to death. After the crowd started breaking up, I could see that they were only going to another area a little further away to watch him being beaten and then forced to take his cross to Golgotha. I watched in horror, wanting to turn my face away from the sight as he was being crucified, but I couldn't. I stared in unbelief that this was actually happening to a man who had never done anything wrong and who had made the lives better for so many. I truly believed he was the Son of God and now this. Where was his Heavenly Father now when all this was happening?

I mourned over the next two days, but my mourning turned to joy and disbelief when I heard that Jesus was alive! He had conquered death! The women that were the closest to him were the first to see him alive. They must have been so excited when they came to his empty tomb and saw the angel and heard him say that Jesus had risen from the dead and commanded them to go and tell his disciples. I was so happy. Jesus was who he said he was! He was our Savior. As I studied the scriptures of the prophets it became clear that he wasn't here to set up an earthly kingdom, as some had thought, but to save a sinful world through his sacrifice on the cross. The suffering he bore started to make sense to me. He was the sacrificial lamb. He was the Son of God!

Thank you Father that we have seasons in our lives when we can focus on you and celebrate your crucifixion and your return to life and are living forever in our hearts. Help us to realize that this is something that we can celebrate just not on Easter, but every day of the year. Thank you for taking our sins upon you and forgiving us. Help us to always live our lives in remembrance of your love for us. In Jesus name, I pray. Amen.

NOTES: _____

_____

_____

"Thank God for tea! What would the world do without tea! How did it exist? I am glad I was not born before tea."
SYDNEY SMITH, A MEMOIR OF THE REV. SYDNEY SMITH

Almond Cookie Bars

8 ounce piecrust or pastry crust (thaw if frozen) or make your favorite crust recipe

Flour for dusting

4 tablespoons of raspberry jam (blueberry would be good too)

4 egg whites

1 ½ cups of ground almonds

1 cup sugar

A few drops of almond extract

¾ cup of sliced almonds

1 tablespoon powdered sugar for dusting

Preheat oven to 350 degrees F. Roll crust out and lay in a 9 X13 inch cake pan covering bottom and sides of pan. Spread Jam over unbaked crust. Use more jam if needed. Put egg whites in bowl and beat until stiff peaks form. Beat in sugar and almond extract and then fold in ground almonds (you can ground almonds by pulverizing in a food processor or buying them already ground or in flour form). Pour beaten egg white/almond mixture over the top of the jam and spread until level. Sprinkle sliced (flaked) almonds over the entire surface. Bake for 30-35 minutes or until the pastry is crisp and the topping is golden brown and firm to the touch. Leave to cool in pan. Cut into squares and sprinkle with powdered sugar before serving.

For extra sweetness, instead of pie/pastry crust, line pan with rolled out sugar cookie dough.

-Week 35-

It is a good thing to give thanks unto the LORD, and to sing praises unto thy name, O most High: To show forth thy loving kindness in the morning, and thy faithfulness every night.

PSALMS 92:1-2

KATIE HAD A BEAUTIFUL SOUL. SHE WAS OUTGOING and brought smiles to everyone she came in contact with. It seems she never had a bad day. From the time she was a little girl, she would wake up in the morning and start her day on her knees before the Lord. She knew that no matter what happened that day, God would take care of her. Even if bad things happened, she would praise God and bow her head and say 'thank you God, I know you are in control of even this,' and then she would turn her problem over to God and go on. At the end of the day, before she went to bed she praised God and thanked him for seeing her through another day.

After she graduated from high school, her life started to change. She had been an honor roll student and was able to get in the college of her choice. She was excited as she packed for her move to school. Her mother and father were proud of her, but sad that their only child was going away to a school out of state and so far away. They didn't know what they would do without their 'ray of sunshine' daughter.

In the afternoon, on the day before they were to leave, Katie and her mom decided to go out to a fancy restaurant. The restaurant had a special tearoom where they could enjoy a special afternoon tea. They decided to do it up right. They got all dressed up in their finest clothes and jewelry and even wore a fancy hat and gloves. It reminded them of the little 'tea parties' they had when Katie was a little girl. The baristas brought them their own personal pot of tea and two beautiful china cups and saucers. Next they brought in a three-tiered server full of wonderful treats. There were a variety of tea sandwiches, scones, cookies, and fruit with a special dipping cream. Wonderful relaxing music was playing in the background. They spent the next two hours reminiscing over all the years she was growing up. As they looked back, Katie realized that even through the difficult times in her life, like the time she was diagnosed with cancer and had to go through radiation and chemotherapy and then when her grandma and grandpa died, she was still able to praise God. He brought her through those times because she knew that he loved her and wanted what was best for her. She knew that her grandparents were with him now and were looking down on her as she made this new move in her life. Before leaving the restaurant that day, they held hands across the table and thanked the Lord for their life together and for what he was going to do with her in the future.

Many years had come and gone, and Katie and her mom would once a year, on the same date, meet together for an afternoon tea and reminisce about how God had blessed them. Only now, another young lady joined with her mother and grandmother to continue in this celebration of life.

Thank you Lord, for all your goodness. Let us always praise you in the mornings, afternoons, and evenings and give you the glory for everything that comes our way. In Jesus name, I pray. Amen.

NOTES: _____

_____

_____

Apple Roulade

Scone/biscuit layer

	4 large eggs
	¾ cup of all-purpose flour
	¾ cup of sugar

Filling

	3 cups of grated or finely chopped apples (grated works best or use pulse setting on blender)
	2 tablespoons sugar
	1 teaspoon cinnamon

Powdered sugar for dusting

Preheat oven to 350 degrees F. Layer cookie pan with parchment paper (important to use this). Peel apples and grate or finely chop them. Drain off excess juice, if any. Add 2 tablespoons sugar and 1 teaspoon cinnamon to apples. Mix well. Pour apple mixture in a rectangle shape layer on parchment paper on cookie pan. Next prepare scone batter by beating 4 large eggs with mixer for 4-5 minutes. Towards the end of beating the eggs, add the sugar. Once the sugar is thoroughly mixed in, add the flour and mix well. Pour batter over the apple mixture, covering completely. Bake in oven for 15-20 minutes until scone layer starts to turn brown. Carefully turn the scone side down onto a clean kitchen towel. Remove parchment paper from the apple mixture side. Using the towel, begin rolling the scone and apple layer into a 'jelly roll'. When finished, trim the ends and sprinkle the roll with powdered sugar. Slice in ½ inch slices.

-Week 36-

And he spake many things unto them in parables, saying, 'Behold, a sower went forth to sow; And when he sowed, some seeds fell by the way side, and the fowls came and devoured them up: Some fell upon stony places, where they had not much earth: and forthwith they sprung up, because they had no deepness of earth: And when the sun was up, they were scorched; and because they had no root, they withered away. And some fell among thorns; and the thorns sprung up, and choked them: But others fell into good ground, and brought forth fruit, some a hundredfold, some sixtyfold, some thirtyfold. Who hath ears to hear, let him hear.

MATTHEW 13:3-9

SPRING, THAT BEAUTIFUL TIME OF YEAR. WARMER TEMPERATURES and bright sunlight and longer days stirs in many of us, a desire to go out and plant something. Whether it's flowers or a vegetable garden, it doesn't matter. Just getting outside and experiencing the wonder of putting a tiny seed or seedling in the ground and watching it grow just brings out the natural person in us. Humans are born nurturers.

During the time of Jesus, it was no different. People always sowed seeds so they could eat or enjoy the beauty of flowers and herbs, so when Jesus spoke of the parable of the sower, he talked to people on their level. But then, as now, there were many people who just didn't understand.

Some took him quite literally and thought he was actually talking about people like the farmers, sowing the seeds. They didn't realize he was talking about sharing the word of God. He was the sower and those that followed him and preached his words were his fellow laborers. Some of the seeds of the word of God fell by the wayside. Those seeds were thrown out for anyone to hear, but if they didn't take the words to heart, there would be no impact at all on their lives, and the words would be lost. Some of the seeds were sown on stony hearts and those with shallow lives. They may have actually heard the words and the ones that did penetrate their minds, were only there for a short while and forgotten a few days later. Still others heard the word and had good intentions of following him, but then Satan came into their lives with the bad influences of others or because of their own weak spirit, and their lives that had so much potential, became unfruitful. Lastly the seeds (or Word of God) that fell on the good soil of the fully committed child of God were able to produce the fruits of the spirit. Some produced more than others according to their depth of commitment. What kind of soil do you possess? Is your heart hardened or torn between the world and God, or do you have a receptive heart and are willing to grow into the kind of person God wants you to be?

Lord, break up my hardened spirit into fine soil that is the perfect ground for you to sow your word. Help me cultivate and nurture the seeds you planted in my heart so that I may bear fruit for your kingdom. As I bear that fruit, let me be the source of the seeds that are planted in other's hearts so that others will desire you too. In Jesus name, I pray. Amen.

NOTES: _____

_____

_____

Chocolate 4-Layer Cake

Cake:

Chocolate cake mix (see list of ingredients on box)

Chocolate Icing:

6 tablespoons butter, softened

2 2/3 cups powdered sugar

½ cup cocoa

1/3 cup milk

1 teaspoon vanilla

Brown Sugar Icing:

1/2 cup butter

1 cup packed brown sugar

¼ cup milk

2 cups powdered sugar

Preheat oven to 350 degrees F. Prepare four 9' round cake pans with cooking spray. Make cake according to directions on cake box. Divide batter into the four cake pans and bake as directed. Cool for 10 minutes and remove from pans to wire racks.

Chocolate Icing: Cream butter. Add powdered sugar and cocoa alternating with milk and vanilla until desired consistency for spreading.

Brown sugar icing: Melt the butter in a medium saucepan. Add the brown sugar and bring to a boil stirring constantly. Lower heat to low and continue to boil for 2 more minutes, continuing to stir. Remove from heat and cool. Once cooled, add the powdered sugar and beat until thickened enough to spread.

Cut the tops off the cake layers to make them level. As you begin to layer, spread the first 3 layers with the brown sugar icing. Lay the fourth and final layer on top. Spread the chocolate icing over the sides and top of the whole cake. Garnish or decorate as desired.

-*Week 37*-

*Whether ye eat, or drink, or whatsoever ye do, do all to
the glory of God.*

1 CORINTHIANS 10:31

KARI AND HER HUSBAND HAD JUST LOST THEIR jobs within a few weeks of each other. Kari had been an elementary school teacher and her husband was an aerospace engineer. They had lived in an upper middle class neighborhood and their two small children went to a wonderful private school. Soon their savings became depleted while trying to pay their bills, as they struggled to find new jobs. With no chance of finding another job and with their money gone, they were forced to give up their home when the bank foreclosed on their mortgage. Then the car company repossessed their vehicles.

If they were a praying family, they would have sought God's favor and his help, but they had given up on religion a long time ago when they were in college. Now destitute, Kari remembered the conversation she had with her new sister-in-law a few years before. Maybe she was right. Maybe she and her family did have one last hope. She called her from a pay phone and told her what happened. Her sister-in-law told her that she should call her husband's parents. If they knew about their problems they would be glad to help. So Kari and her husband swallowed their pride and made the call.

The parents wired money for their airline tickets to come home and with what meager possessions they had, they flew across the country and moved in with her in-laws.

They humbled themselves before them and before God, and then they gave their hearts over to the Lord. A few weeks later, an elderly couple at their church told them that they owned an old Victorian home and tearoom and they couldn't keep up with it anymore. They were planning on retiring and moving to Florida and were looking for someone to take over the business and they could live in the apartment on the second floor in payment for running the teashop.

Although there was a lot of work to be done, it was a wonderful opportunity for them. The tearoom was an astounding success. From the first day they reopened the restaurant they never failed to give God thanks for his many blessings and their new life.

They hung a plaque over the mantel in the main tearoom. It was the verse they found in 1 Corinthians 10:31.

Dear Heavenly Father, thank you for your everyday blessings. We don't always know why some things happen in our lives, but we know you hold the future. Let us always give you honor in all things. Whether we eat, or drink or in whatever we do, help us to always remember to give you the honor. In Jesus name, I pray. Amen.

NOTES: _____

_____

_____

*"The cup of tea on arrival at a country house
is a thing which, as a rule, I particularly enjoy.
I like the crackling logs, the shaded lights, the
scent of buttered toast, the general atmosphere
of leisured coziness."*
P.B. WODEHOUSE

Peanut Butter Fudge

2 sticks of butter

1 cup of smooth peanut butter (or crunchy if you prefer)

1 teaspoon of vanilla

1 pound of confectionary sugar

Prepare an 8 or 9-inch square pan by spraying or greasing with butter and then placing parchment paper in bottom. Place the butter and peanut butter in a large microwaveable bowl. Cook on high for about 2 minutes. Remove from microwave and stir. Microwave for another 2 minutes. After removing the second time add the vanilla and powdered sugar. Stir until it stiffens and becomes hard to mix. Pour mixture into the prepared pan. Cover surface with another piece of parchment paper or cover and refrigerate until cool. Cut into squares and place in an airtight container until ready to serve. It can be stored at room temperature for up to a week. It will last longer if refrigerated.

"Mr. Hanway endeavors to show, that the consumption of tea is injurious to the interest of our country...he is to expect little justice from the author of this extract, a hardened and shameless tea drinker, who has for twenty years diluted his meals with only the infusion of this fascinating plant, whose kettle has scarcely time to cool, who with tea amuses the evening, with tea solaces the midnight, and with tea welcomes the morning."
SAMUEL JOHNSON, 1757

-*Week 38*-

*But continue thou in the things which thou hast learned
and hast been assured of, knowing of whom thou hast
learned them; And that from a child, thou hast known
the holy scriptures, which are able to make thee wise
unto salvation through faith which is in Christ Jesus. All
scripture is given by inspiration of God, and is profitable
for doctrine, for reproof, for correction, for instruction
in righteousness: That the man of God may be perfect,
thoroughly furnished unto all good works.*

2 TIMOTHY 3:14-17

I LOVE TO SEE THE CHILDREN AT OUR CHURCH. They are so full of inno-
cence and delight. It's fun to see them clutching their Bibles to their
chests and holding their parent's hands as they enter the sanctuary. They
are so uninhibited and their little minds and hearts are so eager to learn
about Jesus. It's no wonder that Jesus set a little child down in the midst
of a congregation of people and said to them, '*Suffer the little children to
come unto me, and forbid them not: for of such is the kingdom of God. Verily
I say unto you, whosoever shall not receive the kingdom of God as a little
child, he shall not enter therein.*' Mark 10:14-15.

Timothy's mother and grandmother were godly women. They wanted
to make sure he was taught from a very young age to love the Lord. I'm
sure that they would often sit him down when he was a young child and
would tell them the stories of Adam and Eve and how they took care of

the garden and the animals until they sinned and had to leave. I'm sure as a small boy, he thrilled at the story of Noah and the flood and how he and his family built the giant ship and saved the animals. Imagine his amazement as they told him of the plagues and how Moses led the Hebrews out of Egypt and across the Red Sea on dry land with the walls of water on both sides of them. When they talked about David and how he killed Goliath and later became a great king, he wanted to go out and pretend he was a great leader. Then they told him about Jesus. They told about his birth and the angels appearing to the shepherds and how the shepherds and wise men came and worshipped him and finally they told him how when this baby grew up, people had turned against him and beat him and crucified him. I'm sure he had tears in his eyes when he heard about the terrible death. But then the wonderful women of God told Timothy that this same Jesus came back from the dead and was alive and was living in his heart.

Timothy grew up in this nurturing home with these two godly women who made sure that not only was his physical needs met, but so was his spiritual needs. Timothy grew into a wonderful man of God and assisted the apostle Paul on some of his missionary journeys.

Are you a godly person and are you training the next generation to love the Lord? Whether you are a parent or a mentor, God has given you an important job in telling others about his love.

Lord, thank you for the opportunity you have given us to share your word. Let us not be slack in something that is so important as teaching our young ones about your love. When we worship you, let us be like little children when we approach your throne in love and awe. In Jesus name, I pray. Amen.

NOTES: _____

_____

_____

The Perfect Cup of Tea

1. Boil a kettle of water

2. Warm the tea pot by putting some of the boiling water into it and swirling it and discard the water

3. Add tea: either tea bags or loose tealeaves (1 bag or 1 tea-spoon per person (per cup) and 1 for the pot). You can add more if you like it stronger.

4. Pour boiling water over tea, stir and put the lid on the pot and let steep (brew) for 5 minutes. Make sure the water is boiling so that the flavors fully develop.

5. If desired, pour a small amount of milk into each cup and if you are using loose tea make sure you strain it as you pour. (If you don't use milk, you could add a slice of lemon if you wish, but trust me on this: don't use both milk and lemon! The two don't mix; I learned this the hard way!

6. Traditionally, a bone china tea set is used. Somehow tea tastes even better in a beautiful tea set! However any glass or porcelain cup will do.

7. Add sugar (I like using raw sugar) or other sweetener of your choice, if you like it sweeter. Stir and enjoy!

Later in this book, I will go into the various types of teas and their origins and also the benefits of herbal teas.

> "Drink your tea slowly and reverently, as if it is the
> axis on which the world earth revolves...slowly, evenly,
> without rushing toward the future."
> THICH NAT HAHN

-Week 39-

And he gave some, apostles: and some, prophets; and some, evangelists; and some pastors and teachers; for the perfecting of the saints, for the work of the ministry, for the edifying of the body of Christ: till we all come in the unity of the faith, and of the knowledge of the Son of God, unto a perfect man, unto the measure of the stature of the fullness of Christ: that we henceforth be no more children, tossed to and fro, and carried about with every wind of doctrine, by the sleight of men, and cunning craftiness, whereby they lie in wait to deceive; but speaking the truth in love, may grow up into him in all things, which is the head, even Christ:

EPHESIANS 4:11-15

WHAT DO YOU WANT TO BE WHEN YOU grow up? How many times have we asked our children that? How many times did people ask us that question?

When we were younger the whole world seemed to be ours for the taking. We dreamed of the day when we would be grown up and able to do anything we wanted. We dreamed of exotic careers like being a famous movie star, a famous athlete, a superhero, a prince or a princess. We knew it would probably never happen, but it was fun to dream. Then as we got older and more realistic we still had dreams, but they were based more on reality. We started to explore our options. We still wanted to do something we loved and we started our adult lives pursuing those dreams, but then finally we realized that we would have to settle on something with which we could actually earn a living. If we were lucky, our dreams and our reality would cross at some point, or our jobs would become our new dream.

It is not wrong to hope for a brighter future when seeking a new job or changing our career path. Becoming more based in reality is all part of growing up. Seeking the Lord's will in our career choice is always a wise decision. The Lord knows where we are and what our future holds, but wherever we end up, if we are in his will, God wants to be there. He gave all of us special gifts and talents and he wants us to use them for the edifying of the saints. No matter what we do, we can still be a witness for him. We can serve him as we go about our daily jobs and lives. We don't have to be a pastor, missionary, or a full time Christian worker to work for him. We just have to be faithful. Opportunities to do good things or to be a witness will always be there for us. We just need to be open to his leading.

Lord, help me as I do my job today to find ways that I can serve you. Help me be a witness for you, not just in words, but by the way I represent you by doing everything to your glory. My life may not have turned out the way I would've wanted, but it is the way you planned for me if I am in your will, and I thank you for the opportunity to serve you. In Jesus name, I pray. Amen.

NOTES: _____

_____

_____

"If you have one teapot
And can brew your tea in it
That will do quite well.
How much does he lack himself
Who must have a lot of things?"
SEN NO RIKYU

Friendship Spiced Tea

½ cup plain instant tea powder
1 cup sweetened lemonade powder (e.g. Country Time)
1 cup orange-flavored powder drink mix (e.g. Tang)
1 teaspoon cinnamon
½ teaspoon ground cloves

Mix all dry ingredients in a large bowl and pour into an airtight container (special tea containers can be bought at tea specialty shops. It also looks wonderful in a clear glass container).

To serve: put 2 or 3 teaspoons of mix in a cup and stir in 1 cup of boiling water.

This makes a wonderful gift for your friends, especially around Thanksgiving or Christmas. Put it in a decorative jar or a canning jar with a colorful piece of cloth over the lid and tie ribbon or raffia around the rim and cloth for decoration. If it is a gift, attach a decorative tag with instructions for mixing the tea.

My husband swears by this tea. Likes to drink it all the time, especially in the winter. He thinks it keeps him from getting colds. Can't hurt I guess, it's loaded with Vitamin C. and cinnamon and cloves have a warming effect on the body. Add a little raw honey for extra sweetening to add even more healing power to this wonderful tea.

-*Week 40*-

Remember now thy Creator in the days of thy youth,
while the evil days come not, nor the years draw nigh,
when thou shalt say, I have no pleasure in them.
ECCLESIASTES 12:1

AS AN OLDER ADULT, I FIND PLEASURE AS I watch children at play. It has been a long time since I had their youthful energy and exuberance. I would love to have even a little bit of their 'get up and go'. Sometimes I find myself wishing I could go back to their age and have a 'do over'. I tell myself that if I could do things over I would do things differently. If only I was more outgoing. If only I didn't let things bother me so much. If only I chose a different career path. If only, if only... If only I sold myself out completely to God while I was young!

I don't believe that God wants us to grow older wishing that things were different. Through our experiences, we become wiser and are more able to instruct our children about what they should do so they won't have the same regrets that we may have had. If only they would listen.

When Solomon wrote these words, I'm sure he was growing old. When he was young he loved God. He was the wisest man in the world as well as the richest. He could have had anything he wanted, but through his wealth he turned away from God. Now at the end of his life he was a broken man. He no longer followed God and realized that everything thing in his life at this time meant nothing and was all vanity. Now he was trying to preach to the younger generation that they needed to follow God while they were still young and able to be molded, to conform to his grace and mercy, because if they didn't, when they were old they were less likely to be conformed to God's will. Like him...

I've been very fortunate. Do I have regrets? Sure I do. My life wasn't idyllic. When I grew up we didn't have a lot, but I had a family who loved me. I wasn't a perfect child and I was bullied and teased in school and only made mediocre grades, but somehow I survived those years. I loved Jesus and even though my parents stopped going to church when I was little, I still found a way to go with my friends. Later, church became a big part of my life while I was in the Air Force during the Viet Nam war. After that, I went to college, got married, became a nurse, and had my own children. All during that time, I still followed the Lord. Now I'm in my sixties. I'm pursuing my life long dream of being a writer, and you may have figured out by reading my books, that yes, I'm still following the Lord!

So do I want to go back and change my life? Not likely! All of these experiences have made me who I am today. I'm just happy that I found the Lord when I was young. He helped me get through the hard times and I know he will continue to be with me for the rest of my life.

Thank you Lord for your provisions. Thank you that I have known you as a child, even as I do now. Help me find ways to instruct others in your love, especially those who are younger and newer in their faith. Help me to remember that it's never too late to begin anew and to change things in my life where change is needed. In Jesus name, I pray. Amen.

NOTES: _____

_____

_____

Spiced Milk Tea (Masala Chai)

2 cups water

3 black tea bags or 3 teaspoons of loose black tea

1 cinnamon stick

¼ teaspoons of cardamom seeds

4 whole cloves

Pinch of nutmeg

1 inch peeled and sliced ginger root

1 teaspoon of vanilla

4 black peppercorns

2 tablespoons brown sugar or honey

2 cups milk

In a large saucepan, add the water, tea bags (or loose tea), spices and brown sugar (or honey). Bring to a boil, then cover and reduce the heat to low. Let simmer for about 5 minutes (more if you want a stronger spice taste). Add milk and bring back to a simmer (do not boil with the milk in it). Remove from heat and strain through a strainer or coffee filter before serving. This can be served hot or over ice for a cold drink. Store rest of tea in the refrigerator for later use.

"Though I cannot flee
From the world of corruption,
I can prepare tea
With water from a mountain stream
And put my heart to rest."
UEDA AKINARI

-Week 41-

Beloved, think it not strange concerning the fiery trial which is to try you, as though some strange thing happened unto you: But rejoice, inasmuch as ye are partakers of Christ's sufferings; that when his glory shall be revealed, ye may be glad also with exceeding joy.

1 PETER: 4:12-13.

IN EACH OF MY NOVELS IN MY "WOMEN OF GOD" series, each of my heroines faced challenges through some kind of loss. Some lost family members, some lost their health, and still others lost all of their possessions. Although the stories are fictitious and dramatic, they are representative of things that some people go through in their lives. God didn't promise us that we would never go through trials in our lives. Things are going to happen. Sooner or later if we live long enough, we are going to suffer the loss of a loved one, our health is going to deteriorate, or we may through some catastrophic event, lose everything we own and we may even be abandoned or disappointed by our friends and family members. As Job said in Job 5:6-7 *'Although affliction cometh not forth of the dust, neither doth trouble spring out of the ground; yet man is born unto trouble, as the sparks fly upward'*.

Fortunately, as the children of God, we have a comforter. When we go through the valleys of life, he is there. He will not leave us nor forsake us. He knows what we have to go through. When Jesus walked the earth in human form, he went through all the emotions that we would have to encounter. He suffered hunger and thirst, he had no worldly possessions, and he was sad when his loved ones died and his friends betrayed him. On the day of his crucifixion, some of his closest friends even denied knowing him. He was mocked and beaten and suffered excruciating pain before his death. He even thought that his Father in Heaven had abandoned him. I'm pretty sure that none of us will ever have to go through what he did, but we can be sure that he would be there for us through it all, if we did.

The very next few verses in the book of Job 5:8-11 reads: *'I would seek unto God, and unto God I would commit my cause: which doeth great things and unsearchable; marvelous things without number: who giveth rain upon the earth, and sendeth waters upon the fields: to set up on high those that be low; that those which mourn may be exalted to safety'.*

Are you going through some trials today? Turn all of your hurt and anxiety over to God and draw comfort from the Holy Spirit. That's why he was given to us (see John 14:16-18).

Thank you Father, for your gift of a Comforter.
Somehow our trials and testing may seem difficult,
but we know we will be victorious over our suffering if
we give it to you. I pray for my friends and family who
may need you at this time. In Jesus name, I pray. Amen.

NOTES: _____

_____

_____

"I take pleasure in tea, appreciating it with my spirit and therefore cannot explain why."
SEN JOO

Holiday Tea Mix

2 ounces black loose-leaf tea

1 teaspoon ground cinnamon

1 teaspoon ground cardamom

½ teaspoon cloves

¼ teaspoon ginger

¼ teaspoon nutmeg

2 tablespoons of orange zest

1 teaspoon vanilla powder or extract

Sliced lemon or orange (optional) for garnish

¼ cup of dried raisins or cranberries

Mix all ingredients (except lemon or orange slices) in a bowl. Allow entire mixture to dry (especially if using freshly grated orange zest and liquid vanilla.) This mix will yield about 20 cups of spiced tea.

To make tea, use 1 teaspoon of mixture per 6-ounce cup. If making it in a pot, use 1 teaspoon per cup. Pour boiling water over the tea and let steep for 7-10 minutes for fullest flavor. Sugar or honey can be added for sweetness. Filter out the tealeaf/spice mixture when pouring into cup. Add a slice of orange or lemon as a garnish if desired.

Store the remaining tea mixture in an airtight container until ready for use.

This would make a terrific Christmas gift for your friends or family! Just find a pretty airtight container to put the mix in, add a vintage teacup or teapot and a tea infuser or strainer and a tin of biscuits (cookies). Put them all in a basket for a gourmet gift basket. Who wouldn't love that?

-Week 42-

*But now, O LORD, thou art our Father; we are the clay,
and thou art our potter; and we are all the work of thy
hand.*

ISAIAH 64:8

HAVE YOU EVER MADE ANYTHING FROM CLAY? MOST of us as children
have. I know I did. I use to love to play with store bought clay. It was
fun to see what I could make. I even made things out of mud and let it
bake in the hot sun to dry. Later when I became an adult and took some
art classes in school, I had a class in pottery and learned to make vessels and bake them in a kiln and then glaze them and bake them again to
make them shiny and pretty. The extreme heat from 'firing' them made
them useful and beautiful. Still later, as I developed my skills, I worked
with porcelain and molds and made dolls and other things to sell in craft
fairs.

There are a few things I have learned in working with clay. Until
it is 'fired' in the kiln, it is moldable and can be remolded. If the vessel
isn't perfect, it can be broken and crushed and softened by adding more
water or thinning agents to it and reformed. However, once it is baked
and hardened, it can no longer be changed. After the first 'firing, to set
and harden it, it has to be baked again after the glaze is applied to make
it beautiful and useful. But what happens if the piece is broken after it
is finished? Is it forever useless, only to be thrown away? It all depends.
In the hands of someone who truly loves the piece, it can be mended or

repurposed into another form. Some people have made beautiful jewelry or mosaics out of broken pottery and china. I even saw a picture once of a vessel from the orient that had been broken and 'glued' back together with gold, giving it a special kind of beauty with the appearance of golden veins running through it.

What is the moral of this story? God is our potter and we are the work of his hands. He created us in his image but like the broken pottery, we are less than perfect. Sometimes we have to be broken and crushed to be able to be recreated to become useful to him. In our life we will have trials and sometimes we have to go through the fire before we become beautiful in his sight. We have to be careful, however, to not let those hard times destroy us and turn us away from God. We also have to be careful not to become so hardened that we can no longer be receptive to God's call and will, but even in the end there is still hope. God can still use us even if we are broken beyond repair. We may not be what he first intended us to be, but like the good and loving potter, he still can make something beautiful of our lives.

As you drink from your porcelain or ceramic teacup today, think about the process it took to make that cup. What you are drinking from was once a lump of clay and useless until a master potter turned it into something beautiful!

> *Thank you Lord for your love and for never giving up on us. Thank you for the trials that make us strong and beautiful for you. Continue to mold us, Lord, into a more perfect vessel for your use. Never give up on us Father, we need you to keep changing and growing us into the people you want us to be. In Jesus name, I pray. Amen.*

NOTES: _____

_____

_____

Iced Mint Tea

4 cups of brewed Black or Oolong tea (use 1 teabag or 1 teaspoon of tea per cup of boiling water)

4 sprigs of fresh mint

Juice of 2 oranges and 4 lemons

Minced ginger root (small piece)

2 cups of cold water

Sugar to taste

Ice

Orange or lemon slices (for garnish)

Mint leaves (for garnish)

Brew the tea and strain into a glass pitcher. Crush the mint and add to the tea. Squeeze the juices from the fruit and add to the tea mixture. Add the ginger and sugar to taste. Stir in 2 cups of cold water. Chill tea and juice mixture until cold. Strain tea and pour into a glass with ice. Garnish with fresh mint leaves and slice of lemon or orange if desired.

"In nothing is the English genius for domesticity more notably declared than in the institution of this festival…almost one may call it so…of afternoon tea. Beneath simple roofs, the hour of tea has something in it of sacred; for its marks the end of domestic work and worry, the beginning of restful, sociable evening. The mere chink of cups and saucers tunes the mind to happy repose."

GEORGE GISSING, THE PRIVATE PAPERS OF HENRY RYECROFT, 1903

-Week 43-

Wherefore seeing we also are compassed about with
so great a cloud of witnesses, let us lay aside every
weight, and the sin which doth so easily beset us,
and let us run with patience the race that is set before
us, looking unto Jesus the author and finisher of our
faith: who for the joy that was set before him endured
the cross, despising the shame, and is set down at the
right hand of the throne of God.

HEBREWS 12:1-2

WHILE HE WAS GROWING UP IN TARSUS AND then later on, while visiting areas in the Greek and Roman Empire, Paul no doubt thought about the Olympic races that he had seen or heard about during his travels. He used that vivid imagery when comparing those races to a Christian's struggle with sin and trying to live a Godly life.

Imagine the runner. He or she has trained and exercised and built up their muscles so they could endure the rigors of the race. Trying to win a race without any preparation would be futile because they would give up as soon as the first struggle came along. They may give up, deciding it simply isn't worth it. They just don't have the stamina to deal with the pressure. They take their eyes off the finish line...Jesus.

Then, there are those who are only focused on completing the race. They wear blinders and are self-indulgent and narrow-minded. They don't care about the people around them. They hear the cries of the people, but they ignore them. They plod along at a slow walk or crawl. They may finish the race, but they don't bring anyone along with them. They may still enter into Heaven at the finish line, but there will be no special crowns or rewards awaiting them.

Last of all, there is the totally committed Christian. They are the ones that are dedicated to doing the best they can. They are encouraged by the support of their Christian family and the Word of God and the promise of eternal life and ignore those who would try to bring them down or discourage them. They keep their eyes on Jesus at the finish line and know that only he can save them in the end. As they run, they throw off their cloaks of sin, and remove the shackles that beset them, so they can run freely and valiantly. They long for the victory and are rewarded at the finish line with the crown of life. As they bow down before God the Father and Jesus the Son, sitting on their thrones of judgment at the finish line, they are not ashamed because they know that they ran their best race.

How will you run your race? Are you one of those who quit before they even start or do you plod along and get by with doing only the minimum requirements to get there? Or are you committed to winning the race and bringing others with you and rejoice when Jesus says to you "Well done, my good and faithful servant"?

> *Dear Lord in Heaven, give me the strength, faith and*
> *courage to run the best race I can. I know even in my*
> *weakness you make me strong. Help me to keep my eye*
> *on the finish line and to bring as many people as I can*
> *with me. In Jesus name, I pray. Amen.*

NOTES: _____

_____

_____

Strawberry Iced Tea

2 cups fresh or frozen whole strawberries
4 cups of brewed and cooled tea (white or green tea works well for this)
¼ to ½ cup of sugar (or honey) according to your taste
¼ cup of lemon juice (fresh squeezed is best)

Puree the berries in a food processor or blender until smooth and then strain to remove the pulp. Brew the tea using either 4 individual teabags or 4 teaspoons loose tea. Strain the tea if needed (if using loose tea). Add sugar or honey while the brew is hot. To the cooled tea add pureed strawberries, and lemon juice. Chill in refrigerator until ready to serve. Pour over the ice and use a whole strawberry as a garnish.

"When the girl returned, some hours later, she carried a tray, with a cup of fragrant tea steaming on it; and a plate piled up with very hot buttered toast, cut thick, very brown on both sides, with butter running through the holes in it in great golden drops, like honey from the honeycomb. The smell of that buttered toast talked to Toad; and with no uncertain voice; talked of warm kitchens, of breakfasts on bright frosty mornings, of cosy parlour firesides on winter evenings, when one's ramble was over, and slippered feet were propped on the fender; of the purring of contented cats, and the twitter of sleepy canaries."

KENNETH GRAHAME, THE WIND IN THE WILLOWS

-Week 44-

Now it came to pass, as they went, that he entered into a certain village: and a certain woman named Martha received him into her house. And she had a sister called Mary, which also sat at Jesus' feet, and heard his word. But Martha was cumbered about much serving, and came to him, and said 'Lord, dost thou not care that my sister hath left me to serve alone? Bid her therefore that she help me'. And Jesus answered and said unto her, 'Martha, Martha, thou art careful and troubled about many things but one thing is needful and Mary hath chosen that good part, which shall not be taken from her'.

LUKE 10:38-42

AS YOU CAN PROBABLY GUESS AFTER GETTING THIS far in this book that I have some very definite loves in my life: Jesus, my family, writing, and of course, everything tea! I love the idea of a relaxing day, curled up with a good Christian book, a cup of tea with 'biscuits', and a soft purring cat in my lap. If Jesus were physically in my home like he was with Mary and Martha, guess where I'd be? That's right...I'd be down on the floor with Mary at his feet!

I can also understand where Martha is coming from. I know she was trying to make everything perfect for her houseguest. How many times have I fretted over having the house cleaned and spotless, and a large meal prepared when having company, but was I really doing it for their comfort or for my own pride in having a clean house and a delicious meal for them? I'm sure when my guests arrived, they would have rather had a relaxed hostess than someone who was stressed out and tired and most likely irritable from trying to have the perfect home. Who can relax in this situation?

Through a lot of my devotions and thoughts on tea in the afternoon, the focus is on taking time for yourself, even if it's just a few minutes a day, to unwind and relax with a warm cup of tea and a snack. Other times it would be awesome to have a formal afternoon tea with a group of friends or even a neighbor as you get to know each other better. But whether you are by yourself, or with a group, remember that the best afternoon teas are those that allow yourself to relax and enjoy the moment. Don't stress out and be so busy that it becomes something that you dread to do. You don't have to have a spread of all of the recipes in this book. Most people would be happy with just a simple sandwich and dessert, or just a cup of tea.

Are you a Mary or a Martha? Are you more concerned with keeping up appearances or fellowshipping with your Lord and your friends?

Dear Heavenly Father, help me to be more like Mary and want to fellowship with you instead of being so busy that you are forgotten. Lord I need you to be the priority in my life. In Jesus name, I pray. Amen.

NOTES: _____

_____

_____

Strawberries and Cream Tea

1/2 cup of green or black tea (use tea bag)

¼ cup of pureed strawberries for each cup of tea)

Sugar or honey to taste

Whipped cream (e.g. Redi-whip or other aerosol canned cream)

Strawberries for garnish

Brew tea for 5 minutes with boiling water. Add sugar if desired and the crushed strawberries and stir. Fill cup 3/4 full with tea and strawberry mixture. Fill cup the rest of the way with the whipped cream and garnish with a fresh strawberry.

This would also be good with any other fruit as well. Try it with peaches or blueberries. Avoid using citrus fruits, however, due to their acidity; they would interact with the dairy products causing them to curdle.

The Tea Party
"I had a little tea party
This afternoon at three.
'Twas very small...
Three guests in all...
Just I, myself, and me.
Myself ate all the sandwiches,
While I drank up the tea;
'Twas also I who ate the pie
And passed the cake to me."
JESSICA NELSON NORTH

-Week 45-

*...We spend our years as a tale that is told. The days of
our years are threescore years and ten; and if by reason
of strength they be fourscore year; yet is their strength
labour and sorrow; for it is soon cut off, and we fly
away...So teach us to number our days, that we may
apply our hearts unto wisdom.*

PSALMS 90:9B-10 AND VERSE 12

WALKING THROUGH THE BOOKSTORE, I SEE ROWS AND rows of journals, notebooks, calendars...and ink pens. We have become a nation obsessed with note taking, recording events, journaling, and scheduling our activities. We love to find just the right journals and calendars that fit our personalities. Selling these products has become a huge business! I cannot tell you how many journals I personally have in my home. I have good intentions to record everything in my life for posterity, but alas, after the first few pages, it goes blank. Why do I bother at all with this futile exercise? Even if I did write my life story, one page at a time, everyday of my life, who would care after I am gone? Had I started when I was young, it might have been fun going back and reminiscing as I went through the scribbling on the pages, but it's too late for that now. I do keep a lot of my old calendars and some have important events written on them, but I mainly keep them because I like the artwork (I love beautiful or artistic calendars). What about writing 'to do' lists? Yes, I use to do that too. I enjoyed making the lists and planning my days and then scratching off each job as I did them. They made me feel like I actually accomplished something as I drew a line through each item. On the other hand, if things didn't go according to plan or if something interrupted my carefully planned day, then it would make me frustrated. Then I would have to add the chore to the next day's list and on and on until the list would get so long, I would feel overwhelmed, overworked, and very tired just thinking about everything I had to do! I don't do that anymore either. Now I just prefer to let my days be guided by God. In James 4:15, James says: *'If the Lord will, we shall live, and do this, or that'.*

So am I advocating not numbering our days, or making plans, or writing in a journal? Of course not! Sometimes I wish I would still do that, and maybe someday I will, but whether I do it or not, the important thing for me to remember is that God's plans for my life supersede my own plans because I am his child.

Are you a note taker, a list maker, daily scheduler, or a journal writer? Good for you. You are a person who believes and follows what Moses wrote in his Psalm about numbering your days. But even more important, is that we should begin our days full of praise and worship and thank the Lord for a new day to start again and full of hope that he will be with us this day and his will be done in our lives no matter what we are to accomplish.

Thank you for each and every new day. Help us to make the most of each day as we look for and follow your will in everything we do. Teach us to number our days and apply our hearts unto wisdom as Moses wrote in the Psalms. In Jesus name, I pray. Amen.

NOTES: _____

_____

_____

Lime Iced Tea

1 gallon water

6 tea bags (any type will do, green or black is best)

1 ½ cups of sugar (more or less according to taste)

Juice from 4 limes

Lime slices for garnish.

Mint leaves for garnish (optional)

Boil water and pour into a gallon container over teabags. Add sugar while water is still hot so that it will dissolve properly. Allow to steep at least ½ hour. Discard the teabags and add the lime juice, discarding the seeds. Cool to room temperature and then refrigerate until cold and ready to serve. Pour tea over ice and garnish with lime slices and mint leaves.

"After a cup of tea (two spoonsful for each cup, and don't let it stand more than three minutes,) it says to the brain, 'Now, rise, and show your strength. Be eloquent, and deep, and tender; see, with a clear eye, into Nature and into life; spread your white wings of quivering thought, and soar, a god-like spirit, over the whirling world beneath you, up through long lanes of flaming stars to the gates of eternity!"

JEROME K. JEROME, THREE MEN IN A BOAT

-*Week 46*-

*Thou will show me the path of life: in thy presence is
fullness of joy; at thy right hand there are pleasures for
evermore.*

PSALM 16:11

HAVE YOU EVER WONDERED WHAT HEAVEN WILL BE like? In all indica-
tions from what the Bible says, it will be a beautiful place. Jesus said
in John 14:2 that in his Father's house are many mansions.

John, in the book of Revelation, chapters 21 and 22, heard a message
from God and was carried away in the spirit by an angel to see what
Heaven was like. He described a great city. He saw that the walls were
made of jasper (that is a quartz stone that looks like marble). The city
and streets were made of gold. The foundations of the walls were gar-
nished with several different types of gems. The twelve gates were made
of pearls. There was no temple there because the Lord God and his Lamb
was the temple. There was no need of the sun or moon because the glory
of God illuminated it. There was a pure river of the water of life. It was
clear as crystal as it flowed out from the throne of God. In the midst of the
street and on either side of the river was the tree of life that bore twelve
manners of fruits, and yielded her fruit every month and the leaves of the
tree were for the healing of the nations. When he saw the throne of God
and of the Lamb, their servants were serving them.

When we get to Heaven, God will wipe away all of our tears and there
will be no more death, sorrow, crying, or pain. All things will become

new. God will let us drink freely from the water of life. The best part of Heaven is that we will be forever with Jesus. Everyone there will be a child of God and we will live in peace and harmony. It is going to wonderful and joyous!

What is your idea of paradise? For some, it's some exotic tropical island and lying out on a warm sandy beach and listening to the pounding surf as it washes ashore. Some folks prefer the mountains and walking through the shady forests with the sun peeking through the trees and illuminating the forest floor and looking on in awe of the beauty of God's creation all around them as they listen to the birds singing and watch the other wildlife as they stop, rest, and meditate on the Lord's goodness. Still others find paradise right in their own backyard when they are listening to their children's laughter while they are playing, looking into the faces of their sweet loved ones, and thinking that this is what life is all about. But even though these places and things are wonderful, none of this is going to compare to what we'll see and feel when we get to Heaven.

Thank you Lord for the beauty of this world we live in, but thank you more for the promise of a perfect place called Heaven. While we are looking forward to spending eternity with you, help us to find ways to create a beautiful world for those around us as well as for ourselves. By spending time with you and meditating on your word, we take our first steps into the deeper waters of our everlasting life. Help us to seek out others to bring with us to your throne. In Jesus name, I pray. Amen.

NOTES: _____

_____

_____

Raspberry – Lemon Iced Tea

4 quarts water	
1 ½ cups of sugar (adjust to taste)	
1 pint fresh raspberries	
10 tea bags (green, black, or raspberry flavored)	
¼ cup lemon juice	
Lemon wedges and raspberries for garnish (optional)	
Mint leaves (optional for garnish)	

In a large saucepan, bring water and sugar to a boil. Stir sugar until it's dissolved. Add the raspberries, teabags and lemon juice. Steep for 3 minutes or longer depending on the strength desired. Discard teabags. Raspberries can be left in as a garnish if desired. Pour into a large pitcher or container and chill until served. Serve over ice and garnish with raspberries, lemon slice, or mint leaves (if desired).

"Take some more tea," the March Hare said to Alice, very earnestly.
"I've had nothing yet," Alice replied in an offended tone, "so I can't take more."
"You mean you can't take less," said the Hatter: "it's very easy to take more than nothing."
"Nobody asked your opinion," said Alice."
Lewis Carroll, Alice in Wonderland

-Week 47-

But my God shall supply all your need according to his riches in glory by Christ Jesus. Now unto God and our Father be glory forever and ever. Amen.

PHILIPPIANS 4:19-20

WE LIVE IN A 'GIMME' AND 'GOTTA HAVE it now' kind of a world. So many pleasurable things surround us and we want to have it all. We want to have the most expensive designer clothes, purses, and shoes. We are not content with just having a roof over our heads with heating in the winter and cooling in the summer, but our house needs to be in an exclusive neighborhood with an excellent school system for our kids. We have to have a new car at least every three years. We are up to the very tips of the hairs on our head... in debt.

In Matthew 6:31-34, Jesus said in his Sermon on the Mount: *Therefore take no thought, saying, 'what shall we eat? Or, what shall we drink? Or, wherewithal shall we be clothed? (For after all these things do the Gentiles seek:) for your heavenly Father knows that ye have need of all these things. But seek ye first the kingdom of God, and his righteousness; and all these things shall be added unto you. Take therefore no thought for the morrow: for the morrow shall take thought for the things of itself. Sufficient unto the day is the evil thereof.*

It is nice to be surrounded by beautiful things. I'll have to confess that I'm guilty of wanting things. My current love and hobby is beautiful teapots and teacups, and of course, I want the gourmet teas to go in them. Writing this book has led me into the beautiful world of relaxing teas and everything that goes with them, but alas, except for the part of praising God and reading his word as I do the devotionals, the teapots, teacups, and tea are not going to get me to heaven. Only the love of Jesus can do that. He is really all I need. All of these other things are for my own self-indulgence. So is it wrong to want things? God has built into our hearts a desire for things. If we didn't have a spirit to want more from life, than we would have no hope for the future and life would be boring. In 1 Timothy 6:17-19, Paul stated: *"Charge them that are rich in this world, that they be not high minded, or trust in uncertain riches, but in the living God, who giveth us richly all things to enjoy; that they do good, that they be rich in good works, ready to distribute, willing to communicate; laying up in store for themselves, a good foundation against the time to come, that they may lay hold on eternal life."*

Worldly riches are temporary. What we do for the Kingdom of God is eternal. God has given some people much and others little but it is what we do with what God has given us, is what gives meaning to our lives.

> *Dear Heavenly Father, thank you for what you have given me. Help me to remember that things are just that, things. Possessions can be lost, broken, or taken away from us. They have no eternal value. Only you hold the key to our true happiness and our true wealth, the wealth that is a home in Heaven with you, and the peace of knowing you as my Savior. In Jesus name, I pray. Amen.*

NOTES: _____

_____

_____

Rose Hip Tea

4 teaspoons of fresh or crushed dried rose hips
4 cups of boiling water
Sugar, Honey, or other sweetener to taste
4-6 fresh Spearmint or peppermint leaves (optional)

Variation: add the juice of one lime per quart of tea and served chilled over ice.

Place fresh or crushed dried rose hips in a warmed teapot (always warm a teapot before pouring boiling water into it. It keeps the tea warmer longer and may prevent breakage from pouring the boiling liquid into a cold vessel). Pour water over the rose hips and mint leaves (optional) and steep for 10 minutes. Strain the tea while pouring into a cup or glass and sweeten to taste. If desired, garnish with fresh rose hips and/or mint leaves. Serve immediately while hot or cool in refrigerator for iced tea. This can be stored in the refrigerator for up to 3 days.

Rose hip tea is mild and fruity. It is packed with vitamins and can be served hot or cold.

> *"Who would then deny that when I am sipping tea in my tearoom I am swallowing the whole universe with it and that this very moment of my lifting the bowl to my lips is eternity itself transcending time and space?"*
> D.T. SUZUKI, ZEN AND JAPANESE CULTURE

-Week 48-

Give ear to my words, O LORD, consider my meditation. Hearken unto the voice of my cry, my King, and my God: for unto thee will I pray. My voice shalt thou hear in the morning, O LORD; in the morning will I direct my prayer unto thee, and will look up.

PSALMS 5:1-3

WHAT IS YOUR FAVORITE TIME OF DAY TO talk with the Lord? (A.) Is it in the morning before all the struggles or joys of the day begin? (B.) Is it in the middle of the afternoon when you finally have a breather and take a break with your afternoon tea? (C.) What about at night, after everyone is in bed and you are left alone with your thoughts? (D.) Or are you one of those who say a quick cursory amen before your meals and goes on to talk about other things with the others around you and forgets a half hour later that you even said that short prayer? I've had days that I was (E.) all of the above. The Lord wants us to give everything to him and trust him in all things. We should be in a continual state of worship and prayer, not just at a certain time of day, but all day long.

When I was contemplating writing this book, I wrote a short poem:

<u>Tea Time With Jesus</u>

In the quiet, peaceful, early dawn
As the day begins, new light I see.

My robe around me closely drawn,
I pour myself a cup of tea.
Then Jesus comes to visit me
In this early morning hour.
As he sits across from me,
I pour him too, a cup of tea.
We talk about so many things.
Of joy and happiness,
Of pain and sorrow.
Then as I reach for my cup of tea,
He touches my hand,
And promises me, hope for today
And a better tomorrow.
When as he lifts his cup,
He smiles at me,
'I am with you always,
Think of me
Each day as you sit
To drink your tea.'

*Thank you Father that I can sit with you and talk
to you about anything. Help me Lord to feel your
presence in everything I do all day long, and not just at
certain times. In the morning, I look up to you, as I go
through the day, I seek your guidance in my decisions,
and at night, I thank you for your blessings of the day.
In Jesus name, I pray. Amen*

NOTES: _____

_____

_____

Chamomile Herbal Tea

2 tablespoons fresh chamomile flowers or 2 teaspoons of dried
flowers and leaves

2 cups boiling water

Apple slices (at least 2 thin slices)

Honey (preferred) or other sweetener

Rinse the fresh chamomile flowers and apple slices with cool water. Warm your teapot with hot to boiling water and swish the water around in pot to heat it. Discard the water and add the slices of apple to the pot. Slightly crush the apple slices to release their juices and flavor. Add the chamomile flowers and pour in 2 cups of boiling water. Steep for 3-5 minutes. Strain the tea into 2 cups and add honey or sweetener to taste. The apples give it a fresh and delightful change of taste.

Chamomile is relaxing and it also helps digestion, so this is a good tea to drink right after a meal or before going to bed.

(Caution: Chamomile and other flowers that can be made into tea often contain pollen. If you are allergic to pollen, you may want to ask your doctor before drinking this or any other herbal/flower teas.)

*"The most trying hours in life are between four o'clock
and the evening meal. A cup of tea at this time adds a
lot of comfort and happiness."*
ROYAL S. COPELAND

-Week 49-

And above all these things put on charity, which is the bond of perfectness. And let the peace of God rule in your hearts, to the which also ye are called in one body; and be ye thankful. Let the word of Christ dwell in you richly in all wisdom; teaching and admonishing one another in psalms and spiritual songs, singing with grace in your hearts to the Lord. And whatsoever ye do in word or deed, do all in the name of the Lord Jesus, giving thanks to God and the Father by him.

COLOSSIANS 3:14-17

ANGELA WAS EXCITED. SHE READ THESE WORDS IN Colossians the night before in her bedtime Bible study and she spent the night tossing and turning. Her mind was restless as she formulated an idea about how she could start a new ladies ministry in her church. Her husband had just begun serving as a minister to their small congregation in a small rural community and they were struggling with ideas about an outreach program. As the minister's wife, she felt it was her responsibility to lead the women of the church.

As she tried to sleep the night before she thought back to when she was young and how she loved playing dress-up and having tea parties with her dolls and stuffed animals. It was so much fun to drink 'just pretend' tea, as she would talk about all of her dreams to her 'friends'. Later, as she got older and had real friends, she and her mom would invite them in for a real tea party once in a while. She even remembered one birthday party when she was a teenager. They had a formal, dress-up, Victorian tea party and served beautiful sandwiches and desserts. Her mother had collected wonderful china teacups and saucers and she allowed the girls to use them at the party.

In thinking back on all those things, Angela decided that it would be fun to have monthly or bimonthly tea parties with the ladies at her church and they would meet and discuss what they could do for their community. So with her husband's and the deacon's blessings, she began her ministry.

The other women loved the idea. So before their first meeting they gathered fine china from donations and thrift stores and even her mother gave her the dishes they used so long ago. The ladies decided that each of them would make one dish of appetizers and desserts to bring.

The afternoon tea meetings became a huge success and soon more and more ladies came from miles around. Not only was it a wonderful event for the women in the church, but also through their ministry, they helped a lot of poor people in the area by gathering food and clothing for those in need. As word got out about their ministry, their small church began to grow and many people came to know the Lord. Some of the women wanted to start having the meetings weekly along with a Bible study. Have you ever thought about having this type of meeting at your church? What a wonderful opportunity it would be.

Dear Heavenly Father, help me Lord to learn more of you and use me to be a witness for you. Help me to find new ways of serving you and others. In Jesus name, I pray. Amen.

NOTES: _____

_____

_____

Lavender Tea

3 tablespoons of fresh lavender flowers
or 1 ½ tablespoons of dried lavender flowers.

2 cups boiling water

Honey or other sweetener

Slice of lemon (optional)

Mint leaves (optional)

Prepare teapot by swirling boiling water in it to heat it. Discard water and place lavender flowers in pot. Pour boiling water over flowers and allow to steep for 4-5 minutes. Pour into cups while straining the tea and add honey or other sweetener as desired and garnish with a slice of lemon or mint leaves.

Lavender tea is calming and relaxing. A good eat to drink if you are upset or under stress. It is a good drink to help you relax before you go to sleep at night.

Why not add some lavender and/or lavender oil to your bath water? The aroma is very conducive to relaxation.

"Autumn stars shine through gaps in the wall...He... brews midnight tea by the stove's ruddy light."
FROM A TRADITIONAL TAOIST SONG QUOTED IN THE
CHINESE ART OF TEA

-Week 50-

*And that ye study to be quiet, and to do your own
business, and to work with your own hands, as we
commanded you; That ye may walk honestly toward
them that are without, and that ye may have lack of
nothing.*

1 THESSALONIANS 4:11-12

JESSICA AND KIM WERE ALWAYS TOGETHER. BEST FRIENDS their whole lives, they couldn't do anything without consulting the other. In preschool, they would often go off into a corner to play together and if anyone wanted to join them they would abruptly push them away. In grade school they would sit together on the bus and at lunch and whisper about the other kids. They would sit their books and lunch boxes in the seats next to them so no one else could sit by them. When they got to high school, they became very possessive of each other. When one of them tried to make friends with someone else or get a boyfriend, the other one would do everything in her power to sabotage the relationship. A few times they almost came to blows over breaking up a budding romance.

Then as fate would have it, they became separated when it came time to go to college. They had different goals in their lives and it required them going to different schools. Because they remained friends, the separation was hard on them. They soon grew apart as time went on and were forced to allow other people in their lives. They both eventually married and had their own families and moved far apart to opposite sides of the country.

As they became older, they often thought of one another. They still kept in touch, at least when they remembered to write. They would often reminisce about the good old days, and wondered how it would have been if they would have allowed others into their lives. How much richer their lives would have been if they had reached out and made more friends. Even now, after years of living, they still had difficulty meeting new people or becoming close to anyone.

I don't believe God ever wanted us to be alone, or to limit our outreach to just a few people, but there are times when the best thing in our life is to be alone, like when we are studying his word and trying to listen to that 'voice' deep within us, as he is trying to let us know his will for us. God wants us also to be diligent in our work and minding our own business. He has given each of us a job to do and we need to do it without interference from someone trying to keep us from doing our best.

There is a time for us to come together and a time to be alone. We need to follow the leading of the Holy Spirit to know where we need to be.

God, show me where you want me now in my life.
I appreciate my friends, both old and new, but
sometimes I just need to pull myself away to be able to
concentrate on your word. Help me to know your will
regarding my relationship with others. In Jesus name I
pray, Amen.

NOTES: _____

_____

_____

Pineapple Sage Iced Tea

½ cup fresh pineapple sage leaves

¼ cup of honey

Juice of one lemon or lime

½ cup of pineapple juice

4 cups of water

Pineapple wedge (optional)

Pineapple sage leaf for garnish (optional)

While you are boiling the water, measure out the pineapple sage leaves, packing them into a ½-measuring cup. Juice the lemon or lime and discard the seeds and rinds. In a saucepan, combine the leaves, honey, and lemon or lime juice. Pour the boiling water over the mixture, and steep for 20 minutes or until the leaves are wilted and the liquid is a light golden color. Strain the tea into a pitcher (for iced tea) or a warmed teapot (for hot tea) to remove the sage leaves. Add the pineapple juice to the pitcher or pot and serve either hot (reheat if needed) or cold over ice. Garnish as desired with a pineapple wedge and/or pineapple sage leaves.

Pineapple sage has a minty, pineapple aroma when the leaf is crushed. It can be used in baking or in beverages that call for mint.

"Drinking a daily cup of tea will surely starve the apothecary."
CHINESE PROVERB

-*Week 51*-

To everything there is a season, and a time to every purpose under the heaven: A time to be born, and a time to die; a time to plant, and a time to pluck up that which is planted; A time to kill, and a time to heal; a time to break down, and a time to build up; A time to weep, and a time to laugh; a time to mourn, and a time to dance; A time to cast away stones, and a time to gather stones together; a time to embrace, and a time to refrain from embracing; A time to get, and a time to lose; a time to keep, and a time to cast away; a time to rend, and a time to sew; a time to keep silence, and a time to speak; a time to love, and a time to hate; a time of war, and a time of peace.

ECCLESIASTES 3:1-8

FROM THE MOMENT OF HER BIRTH, SHE WAS special. She learned to walk and talk at an early age. She could read her picture books and memorize simple scriptures before going to school. She was an only child and sheltered by a mom and dad who loved her. In school she had a lot of friends and she was a favorite of her teachers. She always finished her assignments on time and made straight A's. Her family was devout Christians and God seemingly blessed her and her parents. It didn't seem like anything could touch them and their faith.

Later on when she was a freshman in high school her mom gave birth to her twin brother and sister. She enjoyed their antics as they grew and she was fiercely protective of them. Like her, they also grew up in the nurture and admonition of the Lord and with parents who loved them.

But all that changed when she was about to graduate from high school. Her life came crashing around her. She lost her parents and her home in a fire, the twins were taken away, her friends deserted her, and she was hospitalized for depression. Thankfully, that wasn't the end of the story. In my book: Jobella: A Story of Loss and Redemption, Jobella went through many highs and lows in her life, but through them all she gave God the glory and never lost her faith.

In the book of Ecclesiastes, Solomon refers to the fact that throughout life we all will have our ups and downs. It doesn't matter whether we are rich or poor or what our circumstances are. In Matthew 5:45, Jesus says: *'That ye may be the children of your Father which is in heaven: for he maketh his sun to rise on the evil and on the good, and sendeth rain on the just and on the unjust'.*

We all go through seasons in our lives. From the trauma of our birth until the trauma of our death, we all have things that we will eventually go through. God gives us the events in our lives and how we react to those seasons that God gives us, is our gift to him. Have you given him your best in everything that has been handed to you? Do you still praise him in the valleys as well as the mountaintops?

Dear Heavenly Father, thank you for all the seasons in my life. Life isn't always perfect, but you are. When things go wrong, help me to remember that you are still in control and that you will get me through the trials, and when things go right, help me to give you the praise. In Jesus name, I pray. Amen.

Notes: _____

_____

_____

Apple Spiced Tea

2 quarts of water
4-6 teabags or 4-6 teaspoons loose tea leaves (any type)
½ teaspoon of cinnamon
¼ cup of sugar or honey
2 teaspoons of vanilla
1 apple (sliced)
Apple, lemon slice, or cinnamon stick for garnish (optional)

Bring water to boil in a saucepan. Reduce heat and add tea bags, cinnamon, sugar (or honey), and sliced apples. Simmer for 15-20 minutes. After removing from heat add the vanilla. Remove tea bags (or leaves by straining) and apple slices. Serve hot or cold. Garnish with apple slice, lemon, or cinnamon stick as desired.

"...I maintain that one strong cup of tea is better than twenty weak ones. All true tea-lovers not only like their tea strong, but like it a little stronger with each year that passes..."

GEORGE ORWELL, 'A NICE CUP OF TEA,' EVENING
STANDARD, 12 JANUARY 1946

-*Week 52*-

O come, let us sing unto the LORD: let us make a joyful noise to the rock of our salvation. Let us come before his presence with thanksgiving, and make a joyful noise unto him with psalms. For the LORD is a great God, and a great King above all gods. In his hand are the deep places of the earth: the strength of the hills is his also. The sea is his, and he made it: and his hands formed the dry land. O come, let us worship and bow down: let us kneel before the LORD our maker.

PSALM 95:1-6

IN THE BEGINNING GOD CREATED THE WORLD. HE made all things. He made the deep places of the earth and the highest mountains. He made the seas as well as the dry lands and everything that is in the world. He gave us the sun, moon and stars for signs... and he made you and me.

Out of all the countless millions of stars in the universe he made the earth a special place. One that was perfectly suited for life. He made people in his own image and he gave them free will so they could choose to love and follow him or go their own way. He made man a little lower than the angels, but his love for mankind knew no bounds. When man chose to exercise his will and disobey God and commit sins, God, in the moment of his choosing, sent his only Son to come to this world to minister to and heal men's souls and die for their sins.

He gave us voices to sing and praise his name. Do you ever wonder why we sing songs in our worship services before the sermon? It's because the act of singing praises lifts our hearts and sets the mood for worshiping him. Have you ever been in a down mood and then a song comes on the radio that is light and uplifting and it makes you feel better, especially if you sing along out loud? Scientists have discovered many benefits of singing. It exercises our lungs and diaphragm and it increases the aerobic activity of our hearts. It decreases stress and muscle tension and helps us to sleep better at night. It releases endorphins, helping pain to decrease. It can help reduce anger, depression, and anxiety. It makes you more mentally alert and creative. Socially it brings people together

The psalmists in the Bible knew the benefits of music and singing. While David was in King Saul's court, he would sing and play his harp for the king when he was feeling depressed and angry. Often, it would calm him down. The book of Psalms is an anthology of songs that were used in worship back during Biblical times. God in his divine wisdom gave us the hearts and the voices to sing, as well as the songs, because he knew that sometimes we would need to express our praise and lift our hearts in just that way.

Dear Heavenly Father, thank you for the songs you have put into my heart and even though my voice may be lacking in real talent, let me make a joyful noise unto you. Thank you for the perfect world you have given to us and the redemption and mercy of your love. Help us to go out and bring others in to your fold so they can share in worshipping you through praise and song. In Jesus name, I pray. Amen.

NOTES: _____

_____

_____

Elderberry Tea

4 cups of boiling water
4 tablespoons of dried elderberries and/or flowers
Juice from one lemon
Honey or other sweetener to taste
1 cinnamon stick
2 cloves

After the water comes to a boil, add the elderberries and/or flowers (if you use fresh berries or flowers, add 8 tablespoons). Add the lemon, cinnamon stick and cloves. Let the mixture steep for about 10 minutes. Remove the spices and berries/flowers by straining the mixture into a cup or teapot. Sweeten according to your taste with honey or sweetener. Garnish with a slice of lemon if desired.

Elderberry tea is extremely good for you. It is especially good in fighting respiratory infections.

Caution: Do not put any leaves, stems, or roots from the elderberry plant in the tea! These are toxic and can be dangerous!

> *"Having picked some tea, he drank it,*
> *Then he sprouted wings,*
> *And flew to a fairy mansion,*
> *To escape the emptiness of the world…"*
> CHIAO JEN

Types, Descriptions, and Benefits
of the Various Teas

THERE ARE MANY TYPES OF TEAS, BUT ALL of them are derived from the *Thea sinensis* plant. These plants are in the Camellia family. The three main varieties that are recognized by scientists are: *Camellia sinensis*, *Camellia assamica*, and *Camellia assamica, subspecies lasiocalyx.* The variations of the plant depend on the region where they are grown. *Camellia sinensis* is from China (the word "sinensis" refers to something that is native to China). This bush grows to a maximum height of 9-15 feet tall. It is grown in China, Tibet and Japan. It can produce tea leaves for up to 100 years. Camellia assamica (assamica refers to tea grown in Assam, India) is grown in tropical climates. It is referred more to as a tree because it can grow up to 60 feet tall and its leaves grow much longer in length than the species grown in China. The trees can produce leaves for tea for up to 40 years. This tea is stronger and more brisk than the other two and is often used for morning teas. The *Camellia assamica, subspecies lasiocalyx* is grown in Cambodia. It grows to about 15 feet.

Teas have their origins in Southeast Asia and India, but there are also other areas of the world where it is grown, most notably Africa, Madagascar, Russia, the Middle East, South America, Indonesia and Australia.

The difference in the types of teas when they reach your table, are in the way they in which they are prepared and what, if any, scents or flavors are added.

The types of tea and the way they are produced are as follows:

- **White tea:** This is a very limited tea and more expensive. The tealeaves are picked in the bud stage before they are opened. Then they are sorted and cleaned. They are allowed to wither and dry up naturally. The tea is whitish in appearance and produces a pale yellowish liquid.

- **Green tea:** These are non-fermented leaves. The fresh leaves are allowed to dry naturally and then are heat treated to prevent fermentation. They are rolled into balls and roasted again or left out to dry. Another type of green tea is called Matcha Uji. This is green tea that has been cut in small pieces and then re-dried and ground into a fine powder. This is the tea that is typically used in Japanese tea ceremonies.

- **Oolong tea:** This is semi-fermented tea usually made in China and Taiwan. The leaves are processed immediately after being picked. They are allowed to wither and then they are shaken gently to "bruise" the edges of the leaves. Drying and shaking are alternated until the bruised edges of the leaf turn red and the surface of the leaf is slightly yellowed. After a short fermentation period they are dried. Oolong teas are always whole leaf teas and are never rolled into a ball.

- **Pekoe or Orange Pekoe tea:** this is a tea that falls under the black tea category (see next entry). It is made up of both leaves and buds. They have a slightly woody or bitter taste.

- **Black tea:** This tea is fully fermented. The steps involved in making black tea are: allowing the leaf to wither, rolling the leaves up into a ball to release it's chemicals, allowing it to fully ferment (oxidize) and then fired (heated) to stop the fermentation. At this point the tea has turned black and has the familiar tea aroma. The CTC (cut, tear, and curl) method produces smaller bits of leaf particles that are used in tea bags. This is an alternate way to process the black tea.

- **Rooibos tea:** Rooibos tea's scientific name is *Aspalathus linearis* and it is grown in South Africa. Although it's considered more of an herbal tea, I'm including it here because it is processed much the same way as the true teas. The name means red bush and the leaf color is enhanced in the tea making process. It is high in antioxidants and has no caffeine so it is popular with health-conscious people and those who have to limit their caffeine intake.
- **Pu-erh tea:** A dark fermented tea produced in China. It undergoes fermentation as other black teas and is aged. It can be stored as loose tea or pressed into shapes.

Although teas are delicious on their own, many people prefer to drink teas that are scented, flavored, or blended. Some of the classic scented teas are:

- **Jasmine:** Green (most popular), Oolong, or Black tea leaves are placed next to the Jasmine flowers. This is done in the evening as the fresh buds of the flowers are opening up. The fragrance of the flower infuses the tea-leaves. This is done for several evenings until the scent is fully saturated in the leaves. Sometimes the flowers are removed, but they can also be dehydrated and added to the tea blend. Jasmine pearl tea uses the tealeaves and the buds of the flowers and is rolled into a small pearl-like ball that opens up when the tea is brewed.
- **Litchi (Lychee):** This is black tea that is scented with the juice from the Litchi (lychee) fruit. It has a strong citrus fragrance. The dehydrated rinds from the fruit may also be added to the tealeaves. Lychee fruits are very high in vitamins and minerals and the tea is sweet with an almost honey-like flavor.
- **Earl Grey:** Probably one of the better-known teas in Great Britain and North America. It is a combination of a blend

of black teas and the essence of bergamot, a citrus fruit similar to oranges. This tea is best served black without milk or served with a slice of lemon. This is an excellent tea for anytime of the day, especially at an afternoon tea, as it offers a quick pick-me-up. It was named after a popular Prime Minister in England in the 1830's.

- **English or Irish Breakfast Tea:** This is a stronger, more robust tea. The main tea in these comes from Assam teas from India and sometimes Ceylon or African tea is blended in as well. Milk and sugar is added, if desired, to these teas to offset the stronger flavor.

Other teas are named from the areas of the world they are produced. Ceylon tea is a black tea from Sri Lanka. It has a slight citrus taste. Assam and Darjeeling teas come from India and have a full-bodied flavor.

Other flower scented teas might include: lavender, orchid, rose and rosehip, magnolia, chrysanthemum, passionflower, and osmanthus.

Fruit scented teas are very popular in today's market. They include but are not limited to: mint, lemongrass, orange, cherry, strawberry, blueberry, blackberry, lemon, mango and raspberry.

Herbal flavored teas will be discussed more in detail in the next chapter. Herbs also can be added to regular brewed tea or be made into a "tea" with just the herbs.

So what are the benefits of tea?

Going back to the verse I first quoted in my week one devotional in Ezekiel 47:12: "...and the leaf thereof for medicine." It is obvious that God created plants that would benefit man. For thousands of years in the Orient, tea has long been considered essential for good health and wisdom. Now in our days of scientific research, it has been proven what they knew for all those years. The scientists have found that tea may help with cancer, heart disease, diabetes, high cholesterol, weight loss, and it may even have antimicrobial properties.

All teas from the tea plant (white, green, oolong, pu-erh, and black) contain antioxidants called flavonoids. They may help against free radicals that can contribute to cancer, heart disease, diabetes, and clogged arteries.

The caffeine and theanine found in teas heightens mental alertness.

Green tea has a high concentration of antioxidants and may interfere in the growth of several types of cancers including: breast, bladder, lung, stomach, and colon cancers. It may also prevent clogging of the arteries that lead to heart attacks and strokes. It has been shown that it could be beneficial in burning fat, while reducing cholesterol levels. It may also reduce the risk of neurological disorders like Alzheimer's and Parkinson's diseases.

Black tea has the highest caffeine content, so it is great for mental alertness. Studies have shown that it may also be helpful in protecting lungs from damage from cigarette smoke. It has also been shown that it may reduce the risk of stroke.

White Tea has been shown to have the most potent anticancer properties compared to the more processed teas.

In a scientific study, Oolong Tea and Pu-erh Tea were found to lower bad cholesterol and possibly help in losing weight.

So the next time you want something good and nutritious to quench your thirst, forget about the sodas or coffee and brew yourself a delicious cup of tea. There is no downside to what it can do for you. Even the act of preparing and drinking it can have a relaxing effect on you. So drink to your health!

Healthy Benefits of Fruit Infused and Herbal Teas

I WILL BEGIN THIS SECTION WITH A DISCUSSION OF the herbal and fruit teas in the recipes of this book and then go on to discuss other herbs that can be used for teas. Each entry will build on the last, so if a spice or ingredient is listed in a previous note, I'll simply skip it and move on to the next item. For instance, cinnamon is used in several types of herbal and fruit teas, so its benefits are listed only once. There is a caution about herbal teas at the end of this chapter.

- **Friendship Spiced Tea:** Made with instant tea and powdered lemonade and orange drink. Instant tea is made from brewed and dehydrated tea. It has less antioxidants than brewed fresh tea, but it is quick and mixes easily, and works well for this recipe. The powdered orange and lemon drinks, although they are presweetened, do contain 100% of your daily dose of vitamin C. The spices in this tea have health benefits as well. In some recent research, it was found that cinnamon might have properties that can assist in controlling blood glucose levels. It has also been shown in some studies that it has antibacterial and antifungal properties as well. Cloves are a rich antioxidant and are useful in treating colds and infections as well as easing upset stomachs. For those who have to control their intake of sugars, sugar-free ingredients can be used.

- **Spiced Milk Tea:** Ingredients include black tea, cinnamon, cardamom, cloves, nutmeg, ginger root, vanilla, peppercorns, brown sugar and milk. Because it contains black tea, it is high in antioxidants. Cardamom is like a pharmacy in a pod! It is high in antioxidants and vitamins. It has been found to help cancer, heart disease, high cholesterol, urinary tract infections, stomach ailments and gum disease among other things. Nutmeg is considered a brain tonic, and it can also help in indigestion and pain relief. It is useful in detoxifying your liver and kidneys, and it can also be used to help you relax and even be used as a sleep aid. Ginger root benefits include easing indigestion, nausea, lowering cholesterol, and alleviating high blood pressure by relaxing the muscles in the blood vessels. Vanilla is relaxing and relieves stress. It can also help indigestion. Peppercorns are high in antioxidants, vitamins, and minerals, so they are useful in combating certain types of cancers and heart disease. They are also anti-inflammatory and they can also help in relieving sinusitis and indigestion. Milk, of course, has vitamin D and calcium, which is good for bones and teeth. So overall, this tea is an extremely healthy tea to drink for good health.

- **Holiday Tea Mix:** With black tea, cinnamon, cardamom, cloves, ginger, nutmeg, orange zest, vanilla, orange or lemon slices, and raisins or cranberries, this tea has many of the spices and benefits as the spiced milk tea but without the milk and sugar. Orange zest can help control blood sugar and is high in vitamin C. It is also an anti-inflammatory. Raisins are high in iron, potassium, and calcium. They aid in digestion and may help prevent constipation and diarrhea. They may also help to decrease sugar spikes following a meal in diabetics. They are very heart-healthy as well.

- **Iced Mint Tea:** Black or Oolong tea infused with mint and juices of oranges or lemons and ginger root. The only new ingredient here is mint. Mint is helpful in freshening breath, relieving headaches, aiding in digestion, acts as an antihistamine, helps respiratory disorders, and can help in mental alertness and memory. Good tea to drink when you are feeling run down and depressed or having cold or flu symptoms. The added juices with their vitamin C will help respiratory illnesses as well.

- **Strawberry Iced Tea:** Strawberries are full of vitamin C, antioxidants, fiber, and a good source of manganese and potassium. They can help increase good cholesterol and are very heart healthy. This drink is a powerhouse of antioxidants and vitamin C with the Lemon Juice, strawberries and green tea!

- **Strawberries and Cream Tea:** This is more of a dessert drink. Still has the healthy benefits of strawberries and green tea, but it also has the delicious goodness of the whipped topping and sweetener.

- **Iced Lime Tea:** Limes are another super fruit as all citrus fruits are. They are high in antioxidants, vitamins, and minerals and can be helpful in digestion. They are good for diabetics, as they prevent sugar absorption. They can help prevent heart disease. When made with green or white tea the antioxidant levels get even higher.

- **Raspberry-Lemon Iced Tea:** High in antioxidants, vitamins and fiber, raspberries are a wonderful fruit to add to an iced tea drink. They also have anti-inflammatory qualities as well and can help ease arthritic pain. It has even been shown that carotenoids found in raspberries can help prevent macular degeneration. Add this fruit to your lemon-iced tea along with some mint and you have a very healthy drink!

- **Rose hip tea:** This doesn't contain any regular tea and is strictly an herbal tea. Rose hips are the fruit of the Rose plant, *Rosa canina.* The rose hips are usually dried before they are used. It is a powerhouse source of vitamin C, along with tannins, pectin, and carotene. For more benefits from this tea add a lemon slice or mint to add more flavor. Pectin is fiber and it can help in lowering cholesterol and controlling blood sugars. Carotene is an antioxidant and as such can help in controlling free radicals that contribute to heart disease and cancer. It is also beneficial in retinal health and helping he immune system.

- **Chamomile Herbal Tea:** The first encounter I had with learning about chamomile tea was when I read about Peter Rabbit as a child. When he came home and had a stomachache from eating too much in Mr. McGregor's garden and being stressed out after being chased, his mother made him some chamomile tea. Turns out his mother (or should I say Beatrix Potter) knew what she was doing because chamomile is known to have a relaxing effect on the body and it can also be used for stomach upsets. It also works as an anti-inflammatory and analgesic. The apple and honey in this tea helps to add flavor and sweetness to this normally bitter tea. There are many benefits of eating apples. It helps in bone growth and protection from bone degeneration. It can also help the brain cells in protecting against Alzheimer's disease. The pectin in apples can be beneficial to lower cholesterol and help in diabetes and the antioxidants can help prevent cancer. The benefits of using honey are widely known and the closer it is to raw honey, the better. I would recommend using honey in all the teas in place of sugar because of its benefits. It is high in antioxidants as well as being antibacterial.

- **Lavender Tea:** Lavender has long been used as a therapeutic herb that enhances relaxation, whether by inhaling its aroma, or as an essential oil in candles or lotions.

As you make the tea, the fragrance tantalizes the senses. It can help with headaches, stress, and muscle tension, and can be drunk at night to help one fall asleep.

- **Pineapple Sage Iced Tea:** Pineapple is packed with vitamins and minerals. It is high in vitamins A and C and has potassium, calcium, and phosphorus. It is an anti-inflammatory and helps relieve joint pain while building stronger bones. It has beta-carotene, which is good for eyesight in helping to prevent macular degeneration. The bromelian in pineapple helps neutralize acids in the digestive track, helping to keep the digestive track healthy. Pineapple sage can also help in digestion.

- **Apple Spiced Tea:** Apples are one of the healthiest foods out there. There is a flavonoid found only in apples that helps in building up bone density. As with most fruits they can also help lower the chances of getting cancer and helps to lower cholesterol. Studies have found that drinking apple juice can help people with asthma have fewer attacks. The pectin found in apples helps lower the need for insulin in diabetics and there was also a study where it was found that people who ate apples tended to lose more weight quicker during their diet program. See previous entries concerning the rest of the ingredients.

- **Elderberry Tea:** Elderberry tea has long been used by Native Americans to help combat joint and muscle pains. It is anti-inflammatory, anti-microbial, and anti-anxiety. It has been found to decrease the length of time of colds because it does help to clear the airways. It can also be used as a sedative and may help to induce relaxation and sleep. Be very cautious, however, when using elderberry flowers and fruits. Make sure you do not use unripe fruit, leaves, or stems, as these parts of the plant contain cyanide.

There are many herbs that can be used to make teas or tonics. Be very cautious about using any plants that you are not sure of. Rather than getting plants grown in the wild or ones that may have been exposed to pesticides, it is better to go to a reputable herb dealer or grow your own.

The following herbs, flowers, and fruits that haven't been mentioned in my previous recipes can also be used in teas:

Fennel	Lime flower
Nettle	Verbena
Valerian	Dandelion
Ginseng	Licorice
Red Clover	Calendula
Yarrow	Rosemary
Lemon Balm	Vervain
Lemongrass	Oat Straw
Passion Flower	St. Johns Wort
Eyebright	Echinacea
Thyme	Sage
Astragalus	Alfalfa
Bilberry	Hawthorn
Peach	Juniper
Cranberry	Aniseed
Black Current	Hibiscus
Chrysanthemum	Honeysuckle
Mallow	Rose Pedal
Nasturtium	Catnip
Blueberry	Blackberry

I'm sure there are many more than these, but this list contains some of the most common plants. One thing that they all have in common is that they are caffeine free and most of them are high in the antioxidants that remove free radicals from the blood stream, helping to prevent cancer and other serious diseases. Some of them are also a good source of vitamins and minerals.

If you wish to make a tea of any of these ingredients, check on the Internet for their uses, recipes, benefits, and precautions before proceeding.

Herbal teas, as well as regular teas, have been around for thousands of years. Evidence of these herbal teas was found in ancient Egypt and China. Before the advent of modern medicine, with its pills and tonics, people looked for ways of curing their diseases and discomforts. They would experiment with different types of plants and when they found something that worked, they would continue to use it and pass down the information to their descendants.

Herbal teas can be a wonderful alternative for people who can't have caffeine in their diet or just wish to find something healthy to drink. Depending on the ingredients, herbal teas can be either a stimulant, a sedative, or provide other health benefits. Herbs and fruits can be added to regular teas to change up their flavor or add more vitamins and minerals to the tea. Before you use any tea or herb you are not familiar with, please check to make sure it is safe for you.

CAUTION:

If you have any allergies, pregnant, breast-feeding, or have any other health concerns about whether or not you can safely use teas or herbs, check with your doctor. Some teas and herbs, although beneficial to normally healthy individuals, may interact with certain types of medications or be detrimental to certain health conditions. If experiencing any adverse reactions after drinking teas, especially those with herbs see your doctor.

The Afternoon Tea

AFTERNOON TEAS CAN BE PRETTY MUCH WHAT YOU want them to be. It can be something as simple as pouring yourself a cup of tea and eating a light snack to get you through the afternoon while you are waiting on a larger dinner in the evening or an elaborate special occasion consisting of three courses of teas and sweet and savory foods. It can be a time of relaxation and meditation in the quiet of your own home, or sitting outside on your porch or in your garden. It could be a time of special celebration with an elegant spread in your formal dining room or drawing room. Afternoon teas would be perfect for wedding or baby showers or a special birthday celebration. It could also be a good time to invite your neighbors or coworkers by to get to know each other better.

Plan and prepare for your afternoon tea ahead of time, so that at the time of the actual occasion, you can be relaxed. If you are having guests, send out invitations with RSVPs so you know how many to prepare for and then make a follow-up call the day before the tea to confirm their arrival. Many of the foods can be prepared a day or two ahead of time and refrigerated in airtight containers to keep them fresh so you don't have to do everything at the last minute.

When having tea by yourself, it is okay to use whatever kind of cup you want to use, but it is much more fun and elegant to use fine china, whether just for you or for a large gathering. I found that there are ways that you can get beautiful china dishes inexpensively by going to thrift shops, antique stores, and on the Internet. It really doesn't matter if all your cups and saucers match. It's quite fun to put together different patterns and let your guests choose their favorites.

In preparation of the table, cover the table with a beautiful tablecloth, or if you are serving guests in a room other than the dining room, make sure you have tables prepared for them to rest their tea and plates on, covered with pretty linens, of course.

When you are setting the table(s) you will need the following for each guest: A cup and saucer, a teaspoon, a sandwich and/or dessert plate, a tea knife and/or fork, and a linen or decorative napkin.

In the center of the table will be the teapot, filled with hot water, a variety of tea bags or loose tea in a decorative serving dish (along with a strainer and spoon if serving loose tea), the sugar or sugar cubes in a bowl with a spoon or tongs, respectively, a creamer filled with milk, and a dish with lemon wedges. Depending on what you're serving you may also need bowls with clotted cream (Devonshire cream in this book), butter, and jam if scones or tea breads are being served.

The food looks more elegant if served on 2 or 3-tiered cake or dessert stands. It also is a space-saver if you have several varieties of foods to be presented. If the guests are not at the table, it is also a convenient way to deliver the food to them after they are seated.

As the hostess, it is your responsibility to pour their tea. Offer them sugar, milk or lemon. If they want milk, you should always pour the milk first and then the tea. Never use lemon and milk together.

Once the tea is poured, it is time to serve the rest of the food. In a proper and elegant tea this is done in three courses: the first course is the scone course. Scones are similar to our biscuits in America. They can be sweet or savory depending on the recipe. The next course is the savories course. Sandwiches can be served during this course. The sandwiches are usually cut into triangles with their crusts removed; however I've seen them cut in quarters and strips, as well. Quiches, canapés, and other types of appetizers are also served during this course. Finally, the third course is the sweets course. All of the fruits, creams, and desserts are served at this time.

Refresh everyone's tea as needed. Once everyone is served, take your own tea and food and sit with your guests and visit between each course.

Above all, whatever else you do, whether you are a party of one or have a room full of people, enjoy yourself, enjoy your guests, and enjoy your afternoon tea!!!

"Find yourself a cup; the teapot is behind you. Now tell me about hundreds of things."
SAKI (H.H. MUNRO), "TEA"

Afterword

T HANK YOU FOR SHARING THIS LOVE STORY WITH ME. When I started, I had no idea where it was going to take me. I knew I enjoyed drinking tea and I loved collecting beautiful teacups and teapots. But most of all, I love Jesus and sharing him with others. What I didn't realize when I started was how much I was going to enjoy learning about the various types of teas and herbal teas and their history and benefits. I loved searching out afternoon tea recipes and making them my own as well as finding just the right pictures for them.

The devotions were another source of learning and excitement for me. I was amazed at how, when I wrote them, the verses that I needed would just come to mind. It was as if the Holy Spirit was leading me to them. I had to dig a little deeper into Biblical history for some of the Bible stories and that was a learning experience as well.

By the time I finished this book, I had a deeper appreciation not only for tea and the art and beauty of the whole afternoon tea experience, but also what I could do in my own life to make the world a better place. I'm now moved to find new ways that I can serve the Lord, by serving others.

If you are interested in learning more about teas and tea trivia, as well as short devotionals and recipes, I have a Facebook page called <u>Jesus, Afternoon Tea And Me</u>. I would love for you to "like" it. I also have a website that talks about other books that my daughter, brother, and I have written. It can be found at: www.kardeesangelpublishing.com

Other books by D.L. Stalnaker:

Women of God Series:
Book 1
Jobella: A Story of Loss and Redemption
Book 2
Eliza: A Story of Overcoming Limitations
Book 3
Billie: A Story of Dedication and Hope
Book 4
From Tragedy to Victory: Zoe's Story

Coming soon:
Book 5
Kari: A Story of a Prodigal Daughter

Facebook Pages:

Jesus, Me And Afternoon Tea
Kardee's Angels

Author Bio

DEANNA STALNAKER'S WRITING CAREER BEGAN FOLLOWING HER RETIRE-
MENT from nursing in 2012. The novels in her "Women of God" series
have at various times been on select bestseller's lists for Christian books
on Amazon. Jesus, Me & Afternoon Tea is her first venture into writing a
non-fiction book and is based on her Christian background and longing
to share inspiration to others, as well as her love of all things about tea.

She is currently living in North Carolina with her husband and her
younger daughter who is also a writer and a teacher. Her older daughter is married and is beginning her career as a pharmacist. She has one
granddaughter.

Made in the USA
Coppell, TX
05 June 2023

17730395R00148